Stewards of the Mysteries of God

Essays on the Office of the Holy Ministry

by

Rt. Rev. James D. Heiser, M.Div., S.T.M.

*Bishop of the Evangelical Lutheran Diocese of North America
Pastor, Salem Lutheran Church (Malone, Texas)*

Repristination Press
Malone, Texas

First Edition, February 2011

Repristination Press
P.O. Box 173
Bynum, Texas 76631

www.repristinationpress.com

ISBN 1-891469-41-X

THE TABLE OF CONTENTS

FOREWORD

God's Word has much to teach us concerning the Office of the Holy Ministry which the Lord has established for the sake of His Church, but in introducing this volume of essays, I turn, in particular, to a portion of St. Paul's words to the Church in Corinth: "Let a man so consider us, as servants of Christ and stewards of the mysteries of God. Moreover it is required in stewards that one be found faithful. But with me it is a very small thing that I should be judged by you or by a human court. In fact, I do not even judge myself. For I know of nothing against myself, yet I am not justified by this; but He who judges me is the Lord." (1 Cor. 4:1–4 NKJV)

The mediate call to the ministry which the Lord extends today to His servants through the estates within His Church continues to call men to this stewardship of the mysteries. As with all good gifts from the Holy Trinity, the sinful minds and hearts of fallen men have tried hard to bend or corrupt that which the Lord has given; certainly the spirit of our age has done all it can to undermine the whole of Christian doctrine, and that has necessarily required a sustained assault on the teaching office. Far too often, servants of Christ have willing laid aside the responsibilities of their calling to purchase—for a time—some respite from the conflict which necessarily attends the proclamation of the Word. Others, because of entrenched false teaching or poor seminary instruction, have never understood that office to which they were called and ordained. Men have set themselves up as judges of what the stewardship of the divine mysteries should entail, rather than trusting the Word of the One who instituted the holy office.

The following essays have been collected in this little volume because there is a need for sound teaching concern-

5

ing the Office of the Holy Ministry. Certainly the pages which follow are no substitute for a thorough study of God's Word and the right exposition of the Holy Scriptures found in the Book of Concord (1580). This book is not a dogmatics textbook; it is not intended to serve as a *locus* on the ministry. Rather, these essays were written over the course fifteen years for a variety of occasion. Several (the essays on N. Hunnius and C.F.W. Walther) were written in 1994 and 1995 while the undersigned was still a seminary student; the Walther essay became the basis of a class discussion, the presentation on Hunnius' teaching was prepared for a conference. The study of the diaconate was written in 2001 while engaged in coursework while studying for the S.T.M. degree.

Many of these essays were written while the author was still affiliated with The Lutheran Church—Missouri Synod; the travails of that association form a necessary context for much of the content. While the undersigned has little interest in continued engagement in that synod's ongoing woes, it would have been problematic to modify these essays to exclude such references. Thus, the pages which follow are, in the main, set forth here as they were originally presented.

I dedicate this book to my parents, David and Martha Heiser, who brought me to the waters of Holy Baptism, raised me in the faith, and have been a tremendous source of moral support throughout the years of seminary and ministry. Luther rightly observes in the Large Catechism: "The parental estate God has especially honored above all estates that are beneath Him, so that He not only commands us to love our parents, but to honor them." The blessings which the Lord grants through that parental estate are truly a gift from heaven.

Rt. Rev. James D. Heiser
Festival of St. Matthias the Apostle

THE OFFICE OF THE MINISTRY IN NICOLAUS HUNNIUS' *EPITOME CREDENDORUM*: A VOICE FROM THE AGE OF LUTHERAN ORTHODOXY

And it is of advantage, so far as can be done, to adorn the ministry of the Word with every kind of praise against fanatical men, who dream that the Holy Ghost is given not through the Word, but because of certain preparations of their own, if they sit unoccupied and silent in obscure places, waiting for illumination, as the enthusiasts formerly taught, and the Anabaptists now teach.
—Apology, Ch. VII, Art. XIII.13

Introduction

The debate over the office of the ministry is among the most long-lived arguments in the history of American Lutheranism. One might say without too much exaggeration that there are as many theories regarding the source, authority, etc. of the pastoral office at any given time as there are synods. This paper owes its existence in no small part to the author's attempt to come to a better understanding of the issues involved in this debate—no small task given the tone of much of the discussion.

It has been rightly said that "The doctrine of church and ministry is without doubt one of the hottest topics in Lutheranism today."[1] One quickly perceives that this debate

1   John F. Brug, "Current Debate Concerning the Doctrine of the Ministry," *Wisconsin Lutheran Quarterly*, (91:1), p. 28.

often lacks the careful historical study which it demands—'heat,' rather than 'light,' seems the general order of the day. The confessions and the Lutheran fathers, when consulted at all, are simply looted for those statements (in or out of context) which agree with one's position.

This paper aims to accomplish several objectives. First, we will defend the important role which the Lutheran fathers should play in formulating a proper understanding of the Lutheran position on these matters. Second, we will demonstrate the significant place of Nicolaus Hunnius and his *Epitome credendorum* within the corpus of the writings of orthodox Lutherans. Third, we will conduct a detailed examination of *Epitome credendorum's* presentation of this matter, drawing in Sacred Scripture and the testimony of the Confessions and of the Lutheran fathers where appropriate.

I. Hunnius and his *Epitome credendorum* in Context.

A. The Enduring Significance of the Orthodox Lutheran Theologians.

With respect to its versatile comprehension of theological material and the breadth of its knowledge of the Bible, Lutheran orthodoxy marks the high point in the entire history of theology.[2]

It would be a grave mistake for any serious theologian to consign the theology of Lutheran orthodoxy to the limbo of irrelevant and outdated matters that concern only the antiquarian. For orthodoxy not only works under the Scriptures as the only source of theology, but it also is eminently catholic and confessional in its approach to theology.[3]

That the above statements are not universally accepted by Lutherans (let alone the broader visible Church) speaks volumes about the state of confessional, orthodox Lutheranism. It is a sad commentary on our culture, both secular and ecclesiastical, that it is necessary to explain why modern Lutherans should be concerned with the work of the Church's ancient teachers. Historical myopia (shared by Christian and non-Christian alike) is certainly *not* a new ailment in America. An interest in the Age of Lutheran Orthodoxy seems an impractical, quaint antiquarianism not unlike that of

2   Bengt Hägglund, *History of Theology*, trans. by Gene J. Lund, (St. Louis: Concordia Publishing House,1968) p. 303.
3   Robert Preus, *The Theology of Post-Reformation Lutheranism*, (St. Louis: Concordia Publishing House, 1970) 2 vols., vol. 1, p. 35.

people who reenact famous battles of the Civil War in a society steeped in materialism, individualism and a universalistic view of religion. There is little that can be said briefly about such an attitude here, for it is either rooted in a disinterest in (or even contempt for) all things ancient or it springs from viewing Lutheranism as one of many ancient errors best forgotten.

Several other groups of critics must be taken more seriously. Some theologians believe such a focus on Orthodox Lutheranism bespeaks a lack of creativity: "Can't you think for yourselves?" One example of this point of view is given by Benjamin Kurtz, an ally of S.S. Schmucker:

> The Fathers—who are the 'Fathers'? They are the *children;* they lived in the *infancy* of the Church, in the early dawn of the Gospel day. John the Baptist was the greatest among the prophets, and yet he that was least in the Kingdom of God, in the Christian Church was greater than he. He probably knew less, and that little less distinctly than a Sunday-school child, ten years of age, in the present day. Even the apostle Peter, after all the personal instructions of Christ, could not expand his views sufficiently to learn that the Gospel was to be preached to the Gentiles, and that the Church of Christ was to compass the whole world. A special miracle was wrought to remove his prejudices and convince him of his folly. Every well-instructed Sunday-school child understands this thing without a miracle, better than Peter did. Who, then, are 'the Fathers'? They have become the Children; they *were* the Fathers compared with those who lived in the infancy of the Jewish dispensation; but, compared with the present and advanced age, they are the Children, and the learned and pious of the nineteenth century are the Fathers. We are *three hundred years older* than Luther and his noble coadjutors, and *eighteen hundred years older* than the primitives; theirs was the age of infancy and adolescence, and ours that of full-grown adult manhood. *They* were the *children; we* are the *fathers;* the tables are turned.[4]

---

4   quoted in Adolph Spaeth's *Charles Porterfield Krauth*, (New York: The Christian Literature Company, 1898) vol. 1, 2 vols., p. 344-345.

Others demand we form our views on the basis of Scripture without taking notice of the historic witnesses (FC Ep Introduction.2, 8). As one recent writer opined: "Unless there is agreement on what Scripture says about the matter [i.e. the ministry], little progress can be made by debating interpretations of the Confessions, historical precedents, and contemporary practice,"[5] missing the point of a *quia* subscription: that the Confessions are the witness regarding what *Lutherans* believe. For the former, the attitude is sometimes rooted in a perceived need for the Church to change her teaching to meet changing times—perhaps utilizing the 'discoveries' of critical scholarship. We believe C.F.W. Walther offered an answer to such critics which stands as well today as it did 130 years ago:

> To let what has already been given the church lie unused, so that we ourselves might be "creatively" active, could be motivated on our part by nothing but dreadful ingratitude and arrogance. This would be to "despise prophesying" (1 Thessalonians 5:20) and for "the spirits of prophets" to refuse to be "subject to prophets" (1 Corinthians 14:32). If men like Melanchthon, Brenz, Chemnitz, John Gerhard wanted to be nothing but Luther's pupils and openly acknowledged that they knew they owed to him next to Scripture, and had learned it from him, who are we to deny and conceal our place as pupils and strive to play the role of masters! "All things are yours," says the apostle, "whether Paul or Apollos or Cephas or the world" (1 Corinthians 3:21-22), and we may and must add, "whether Luther or Melanchthon, whether Chemnitz or Gerhard" [could we add Nicolaus Hunnius?] and we should or would regard and treat this divinely given property as strange goods!? Or is it already truly ours if we have it only on our bookshelves? All gifts, the gift through the Spirit to utter wisdom and knowledge, the gift of prophecy, the gift of being able to distinguish between spirits, the gift of interpreting tongues, etc., gifts which God

---

5   Brug, p. 43.

distributed so lavishly 300 and 200 years ago, all were given "for the common good" of the church in all places and all succeeding times (1 Corinthians 12:7-10)—and we should or would keep these gifts locked up unused!? Or, while we should not seek anything different from what the orthodox church has already discovered, are we to seek it once again? Are we only to tread the same path our old teachers trod in the certain hope that we shall then arrive at the same goal and achieve the same results? Foolish thought! ... It is therefore futile and even sacrilegious to attempt virtually to coerce God into repeating the gracious visitation which He granted the church 300 years ago, repeat it because people do not want to receive the gifts through God's chosen vessels whom He once endowed but, like them, want to obtain them as a fruit of their own searching.[6]

The threat which such "creativity" poses to our Church also remains unchanged:

...frequently rationalists ... know our church's teachings better and present it more correctly than theologians who claim not only to report that teaching historically ... but also to transmit it as its *advocates*. ... And with what unfeigned aversion are teachings rejected as thoroughly unlutheran, unchurchly, as fanatical, or even as papistic errors when they are actually fundamental teachings of the Lutheran reformation of the church![7]

American Lutheranism offers many proofs of the accuracy of this assessment, whether one looks at the theology of S.S. Schmucker or the myriad of teachers floating around in Lutheran circles today.

We do well to consider God's word in contemplating the words of the fathers: "Consequently, you are no longer foreigners and aliens, but fellow citizens with God's people and

6   Editorials from "Lehre und Wehre," trans. by Herbert J.A. Bouman, (St. Louis: Concordia Publishing House, 1981), p. 106-107. [Foreword to 1862 Volume: Do We Lack Creative Activity?]
7   ibid., p. 108.

members of God's household, built on the foundation of the apostles and prophets, with Christ Jesus Himself as the chief cornerstone. In Him the whole building is joined together and rises to become a holy temple in the Lord." (Eph. 2:20-21 NIV) To believe in the holy catholic and apostolic Church means to profess unity with the whole Church throughout the ages. Although the voices of some of the faithful may not resonate as clearly in our age, they still speak to us today, rebuking at one time, encouraging at another. Thus a Lutheran theologian such as Martin Chemnitz could proclaim regarding one of the great theological questions of his day:

> I decided that the safest way to educate and remedy my own simplicity would be to consult the fathers of the church who, in the times of pristine purity and learning directly after the apostles, were active in expounding this subject publicly and with characteristic diligence, and to hear them as they conferred among themselves and shared their well-considered and pious opinions on the basis of God's Word. For in this way, like Gregory's pygmies sitting on the shoulders of giants, we can more easily and correctly form a judgment on the basis of God's Word concerning this difficult question, we can acquiesce with more conviction to sound and simple teaching and we can more safely escape the danger of falling.[8]

It is the operating principle of this paper that Chemnitz' approach will serve us equally well today as we consider one of today's most contended articles of faith—the article regarding the office of the ministry.

B. An Overview of the Life and Work of Nicolaus Hunnius.

Nicolaus Hunnius (1585-1643) was the third son of Aegidius Hunnius (1550-1603), another notable orthodox

---

8   *The Two Natures in Christ*, trans. by J.A.O. Preus, (St. Louis: Concordia Publishing House, 1971) p. 19.

theologian. An instructor in philosophy and theology by the age of 24, Hunnius went on to receive his doctorate in 1612 and was called by the Elector of Saxony to serve as Superintendent (Bishop) of Eilenburg.[9]

Hunnius returned to academia in 1617 when the Elector of Saxony called him to the University of Wittenberg to fill the vacancy left by the death of Leonard Hütter (1563-1616).[10] González seems to imply this return to Wittenberg epitomizes a certain theological inbreeding within orthodox Lutheran circles:

> [Aegidius Hunnius] was the father of Nikolaus Hunnius, ... This is significant, for it has been pointed out that during the period of Lutheran orthodoxy the main chairs of theology were occupied by veritable dynasties, and that theology became an occupation passed from father to son, as any other trade.[11]

Such reasoning is, however, dubious at best. First of all, Aegidius had been dead for approximately fourteen years when Nicolaus was called back to Wittenberg. Secondly, Hunnius had held his doctorate and been a Superintendent for five years before his call to fill Hütter's chair. (One might more fruitfully ask why Elector John George I (1585-1656) was so impressed by Hunnius that he called him as Superintendent and then as professor—two offices which required rather different abilities and temperament.) Thirdly, Hunnius' tenure at Wittenberg was brief enough—six years—before his call as Superintendent of Luebeck that charges of dynasty-making ring hollow. Even when added to the 1609-1612 period of teaching, Nicolaus' nine years in academia is a secondary aspect of his work when compared to roughly a quarter of a century in the office of Superintendent.

9   Arthur Carl Piepkorn, "Hunnius, Father and Son," in *The Encyclopedia of the Lutheran Church*, ed. by Julius Bodensieck, (Minneapolis: Augsburg Publishing House, 1965), 3 vols., vol. 2, p. 1065.

10   ibid.

11   in *A History of Christian Thought*, (Nashville: Abingdon, 1975) 3 vols., vol. 3, p. 250.

The most fruitful years of Nicolaus Hunnius' ministry appear to be those which he spent as Superintendent of the Hanseatic city of Luebeck. Indeed, it was after his call to Luebeck in 1623 that the bulk of Hunnius' written work was published, including his *Epitome credendorum* (1625), *Apostasia ecclesiæ Romanæ* (1632) and his *Diaskepsis theologica* (1626).[12] Two of these works, *Diaskepsis theologica* and *Epitome credendorum*, constitute Hunnius' most enduring academic contribution to orthodox Lutheranism. It is in his *Diaskepsis theologica* that Hunnius sets forth, for the first time in Lutheran orthodoxy, the distinction between fundamental and nonfundamental articles of doctrine to show "that there is fundamental disagreement between Lutherans and Calvinists."[13] Hägglund maintains that this distinction of articles is the development for which Nicolaus Hunnius is best known, "the idea that only certain points of doctrine, and not the entire content of Scripture, ought to be looked upon as necessary to salvation and as constituting the theological position."[14] Of course, by making this distinction Hunnius is doing little more than giving a name to the understanding at work in Luther's catechism, which Luther describes as "a compend and brief summary of all the Holy Scriptures" (First Preface, LC.18)[15]— that is, of the central teachings of Sacred Scripture.

Epitome credendorum also offers a valuable contribution to Lutheran doctrine by its presentation of the *ordo salutis*. According to Hunnius, the order of salvation consists of call, repentance, justification, conversion, renewal, regeneration and union with Christ. This feature of *Epitome credendorum* "became a common procedure among the later dogmaticians."[16]

---

12   Piepkorn, p. 1066.
13   Robert Preus, p. 56.
14   Hägglund, p. 304.
15   Jacobs, p. 386.
16   Robert Preus, p. 56.

However, Hunnius' endeavors in Luebeck were hardly limited to writing. Hunnius "revitalized the somewhat moribund *Ministerium tripolitanum* of Luebeck, Hamburg and Lueneburg in order to mount a combined offensive against the three enemies of Lutheranism in these North German mercantile communities: the ... enthusiasts; the increasingly large Reformed communities; and the Roman Catholic missionaries."[17] Additionally, Hunnius carried out numerous other reforms of the church in Luebeck which destroy the myth of 'dead' orthodoxy:

> He reinstituted individual announcement for Holy Communion and regular catechetical examinations; defended the *regimen ecclesiasticum* of his clergy against the council's encroachments; proposed that the city engage a director of religious education; boldly attacked the vices of his Luebeck parishioners; promoted education; and founded an organization for the relief of clergymen's widows and orphans.[18]

There is much here which parallels Martin Chemnitz' labors in Braunschweig roughly fifty years before: the concern for theological education for clergy and laity alike, the support for the families of the clergy, and the defense of the clergy against interference in its God-given responsibilities all bespeak, when coupled with his proclamation and defense of the faith, a soul which rightly understood, and faithfully carried out, the office to which he had been called.[19]

C. The Enduring Place of Hunnius'
Epitome credendorum in Lutheran Theology.

Although virtually forgotten today, the *Epitome credendorum* was long-recognized as a highly significant work, and its influence lingering for at least 245 years. First

---

17   Piepkorn, p. 1065-1066.
18   ibid., p. 1066.
19   cf. J.A.O. Preus, *The Second Martin*, (St. Louis: Concordia Publishing House, 1994), p. 15, 132.

published in 1625, the present author has located German editions published as late as 1870. Indeed, *Epitome credendorum* was "a perennially popular lay dogmatics that went through some twenty editions by 1870 and was translated into Danish, Swedish, Latin, Dutch, Polish, and finally into English..."[20] It should also be kept in mind that the English translation, published in Nuremberg in 1847, was possibly the first complete dogmatics work of seventeenth century orthodoxy to be translated into English.[21]

Epitome Credendorum was written for the specific task of conveying the theology of Lutheran orthodoxy to the laity. As Gonzalez observes, "Hunnius also helped popularize Lutheran orthodoxy among the laity through the publication of his *Summary of Those Things Which Are to Be Believed*, which he wrote in German and soon became one of the most widely read religious treatises of its time"[22]—an assertion verified by the publication data given above.

We close by observing that C.F.W. Walther recommended three works from the Age of Orthodoxy in his Lutheran Theological Library for Pastors: Johann Gerhard's *Loci Theologici*, J.W. Baier's *Compendium*, and Nicolaus Hunnius' *Glaubenslehre*, that is, his *Epitome credendorum*.[23]

---

20   Piepkorn, p. 1066.

21   Leonard Hütter's *Compend of Lutheran Theology* was not published in English until 1868 (Trans. by H.E. Jacobs and G.F. Spieker [Philadelphia: The Lutheran Book Store, 1868]). It was observed in the translators' preface to the *Compend...*: "No work of like character has appeared in the English language, except Gottheil's translation of *Hunnius' Epitome Credendorum*, published some twenty years ago in Germany, but now out of print." (p. vi)

22   Gonzalez, p. 252-253. See also Robert Preus: "His second theological work of importance is his *Epitome Credendorum* (1625), which became very popular also among the laity, as a brief and readable summary of the Christian faith." (p. 56.) Hägglund (p. 304) concurs.

23   *Lehre und Wehre*, vol. 1, p. 264 and 341 as cited by F. A. Schmidt in "Intuitu Fidei," *The Error in Modern Missouri: Its Inception, Development, and Refutation*, trans. R.C.H. Lenski, (Columbus: Lutheran Book Concern, 1897) ed.

II. The Office of the Ministry as Presented in Hunnius' *Epitome credendorum*.

Hunnius begins his treatment of the Office of the Ministry with two general observations. First, a definition: "The holy ministry is an office, instituted by God, in which He has set aside from the rest of men certain persons, whose duty it is, by His authority to preach His word, to spend the Sacraments, to lead those who are committed to them unto Christ, and to build them up unto eternal life."[24] Second, "Although God might have been able to teach, direct and govern men without any means whatsoever, yet has it please Him, to employ certain men for the purpose of carrying out His designs. This arrangement which has been made for the furtherance of our Salvation, we have now to consider more fully."[25] Regarding the first (which serves as a synopsis of the chapter), it is clear that Hunnius is not speaking of some vague 'ministry' given to all believers but rather that he is writing concerning the pastoral office. The second observation makes several key points: (1) that the pastoral office is a God-ordained means for teaching, directing and governing His people, and (2) that this office has been established for the sake of our salvation. Hunnius' treatment of these points will be expanded below.

A. Names Applied to the Office.

This brief section consists largely of a compilation of New Testament terms used to describe the pastoral office. Hunnius' focus here centers on the three-fold distinction of minister (servant), elder, and bishop. Hunnius believes

by George H. Schodde, p. 441.

24   Nicolaus Hunnius, *Epitome credendorum*, (hereafter Ec) trans. by Paul Edward Gottheil (Nuremberg: U.E. Sebald, 1847), p. 230.

25   Ec, p. 230, ¶ 746.

the term elder was most likely applied to ministers "who had been longest members of the Church and consequently had more Christian experience than the rest;..."[26] Hunnius' remarks concerning the bishops, however, are more pointed: "Although in the Romish Church this title signifies a very high station in the Church, yet in the scriptural sense, it is intended to denote nothing more than a *teacher* or *minister* of the Christian Church;..."[27] Hunnius clearly holds to the Lutheran understanding of the *one* office, within which such grades of pastors are not mandated by divine authority (see Treatise.63-65, for example). This fact must be kept in mind when we later examine the section "Different Orders among Ministers."

B. The Nature of this Office.

Hunnius is concerned with two points in his discussion of the pastoral office: (1) the purpose for which God has instituted it, and (2) the means by which this purpose is brought about. Hunnius' treatment of the first point is brief and direct: "This office has been instituted in order that by it men might be made fit for eternal salvation."[28] The wording is essentially that used in *Augustana* V: "That we may obtain this faith, the Office of Teaching the Gospel and administering the Sacraments was instituted."[29] (¶ 1) While some modern Lutherans attempt to apply Article V to the labors of the entire priesthood of believers, for Hunnius this "office" is not a general office belonging to all Christians but rather: "The holy ministry is an office, instituted by God, in which He has set aside from the rest of men certain persons, whose duty it is, by His authority to preach His word, to spend the Sacraments, to lead those who are committed to them unto

---

26   ibid., p. 230, ¶ 748.
27   ibid., p. 230-231, ¶ 749.
28   ibid., p. 231, ¶ 751.
29   Jacobs, p. 38.

Christ, and to build them up unto eternal life"[30]—AC V and AC XIV refer to the same office, the pastoral office. Hunnius teaches that the means of grace come to us primarily through the office of the ministry.

Hunnius was quite adamant that God does not work this union apart from the means which He established: revelations, visions, nature, human wisdom, angels and extrabiblical traditions are all rejected. Hunnius observed:

> But it is to be remembered that God is not now anymore speaking to us in diverse manners, Hebr. 1,1; that with regard to matters of faith and salvation God never taught His people by extraordinary revelations, but that for this purpose He has ordained the office of ministry, which was exercised by Prophets, priests, and the holy scriptures. We are therefore not entitled to expect God to teach us without any means whatsoever.[31]

Hunnius firmly maintained that the ministry and the Holy Scriptures are the two channels through which God works. Again: "The manner in which God teaches mankind, is of a twofold description; he teaches them *by means of men* and by *His word*, which the Prophets and Apostles have reduced to writing."[32] Finally, "From all this it is evident, that God teaches men and calls them to His kingdom by means of men, whom He chooses to employ for this purpose. It is the duty of these ministers to preach the word of God and to teach in accordance with the same, so that they do not deviate from it. .."[33]

Hunnius was not alone in this understanding of AC V. As Leonard Hütter (d. 1616) wrote in his *Compend of Lutheran Theology*: "2. *For what purpose was the office of the ministry instituted?* In order that we might obtain faith, the ministry

---

30   Ec, p. 230.
31   Ec, p. 176, ¶602.
32   Ec, p. 178, ¶ 607.
33   Ec, p. 179, ¶ 609.

of teaching the Gospel and administering the sacraments was instituted..."[34] Hütter's brief (four page!) *locus* on the ministry works from the assumption that when one speaks of the ministry, one is only speaking of the called pastor. Again, the purpose for the office is "that we might obtain faith..." Again, as Baier observes:

> For the collection and preservation of the Church it is necessary that certain men discharge the office of preaching the Word and administering the Sacraments; in order that, through these means, faith may be conferred upon men, and when conferred may be strengthened and increased. And this is the office which is called the ministry of the Church.[35]

Martin Chemnitz also works from the understanding that the purpose of the office is to publicly bring the means of grace to Christians—a work which is not entrusted to all. Chemnitz offers a very clear explanation of this work of the ministry in his *Enchiridion*:

> *But all believers are called priests, Rv. 1:6; 5:10; 1 Ptr 2:9. Have all, therefore, a general call to the ministry?*
>
> All we who believe are indeed spiritual priests, but we are not all teachers. 1 Co 12:29-30; Eph 4:11-12. And Peter explains himself: All Christians are priests—not that all should function without difference in the ministry of the Word and of the Sacraments, without a special call, but that they should offer spiritual sacrifices. Ro 12:1; Heb 13:15-16.
>
> *Yet all Christians have a general call to proclaim the virtues of God, 1 Ptr 2:9, and especially family heads, to instruct their households, Dt. 6:7; 1 Co 14:35.*
>
> It is true that all Christians have a general call to proclaim the Gospel of God, Ro 10:9, to speak the Word of God among themselves, Eph 5:19; to admonish each other from the Word of God, Cl 3:16; to reprove, Eph 5:11 [and] Mt 19:15; [and] to comfort, 1 Th 4:18. ... But the public ministry of the Word and of the Sacraments in the church is not

---

34   p. 140.

35   cited in Heinrich Schmid, *Doctrinal Theology of the Evangelical Lutheran Church*, trans. by Charles A. Hay and Henry E. Jacobs, (Minneapolis: Augsburg Publishing House, 1961?) 3rd ed. rev., p. 606.

entrusted to all Christians in general, as we have already shown, 1 Co 12:28; Eph 4:12. For a special or particular call is required for this, Ro 10:15.

For what reasons is it so very important that a minister of the church have a legitimate call?

One must not think that this is done by human arrangement or only for the sake of order; but there are many weighty reasons, consideration of which teaches many things and is very necessary for every minister of the church.[36]

This having been said about the *purpose* of the ministry—that sinners would be brought to saving faith in Christ Jesus—what do Hunnius and the other Orthodox Lutherans believe to be the *means* by which this purpose is brought about? Hunnius identifies three means through which this work "is done

I. *by teaching,*

II. *by the dispensing of the sacraments,* and

III. *by church discipline.*"[37]

Of course, Lutherans have become accustomed to speaking of the work of the ministry in a two-fold way: teaching the Word and administering the Sacraments. This is the division, for example, which is found in AC V and AC XIV. This having been said, however, Hunnius' three-fold description is not without confessional precedent. As we read in AC XXVIII, "the power of the Keys, or the power of the bishops, according to the Gospel, is a power or command of God, to preach the Gospel, to remit and retain sins, and to administer sacraments." (¶ 5)[38] Again, we read in the Apology:

Therefore the bishop has the power of the order, *i.e.* the

---

36   Martin Chemnitz, *Ministry, Word, and Sacraments*, ed. and trans. by Luther Poellot, (St Louis: Concordia Publishing House, 1981), p. 29. (hereafter *Enchiridion.*)

37   Ec, p. 231, ¶ 751.

38   *The Book of Concord* (Philadelphia: General Council Publication Board, 1919) ed. by Henry Eyster Jacobs, p. 61. (Hereafter noted as Jacobs.)

ministry of the Word and sacraments; he has also the power of jurisdiction, *i.e.* the authority to excommunicate those guilty of open crimes, and again to absolve them if they are converted and seek absolution. Nor indeed have they power tyrannical, *i.e.* without law; or regal, *i.e.* above law; but they have a fixed command and a fixed Word of God, according to which they ought to teach, and according to which they ought to exercise their jurisdiction. ... And they have the Word, they have the command, how far they ought to exercise jurisdiction, viz. if any one would do anything contrary to that Word which they have received from Christ. (Art. XXVIII.13-14)[39]

Melanchthon, the author of the Apology, continued to express this understanding of the work of the office. As we read in the 1555 edition of the *Loci communes*: "... the *keys* are a command of God to preach the divine word, to administer the holy sacrament, to forgive sin in general and in particular, to ordain servants of the Church, to banish the disobedient if they persist in open depravity, and to absolve and release them if they turn and desire absolution."[40] Chemnitz, Gerhard, Quenstedt and Hollaz follow the same three-fold division.[41]

The first work of the office, teaching, is carried out in two ways: (1) proclamation of the Word of God, and (2) "godly walk and conversation."[42] Proclamation consists of Law and Gospel—"This doctrine having been properly preached unto the hearers, produces that saving faith by which they may be justified before God and made partakers of eternal

39   Jacobs, p. 297.
40   *Melanchthon on Christian Doctrine: Loci communes 1555*, trans. and ed. by Clyde L. Manschreck, (New York: Oxford University Press, 1965), p. 255. Again, the keys are not an illocal power for Melanchthon, but "In Scripture the word 'keys' refers to a household government" which are the preachers or bishops. (see p. 255)
41   *Enchiridion*, p. 26, Schmid, p. 606-607, *The Holy Ministry*, trans. and ed. by Luther Poellot, (Fort Wayne: Concordia Theological Seminary Press, 1991) p. 5, and Schmid, p. 607, respectively.
42   Ec, p. 231, ¶ 752.

Salvation."[43] Hunnius does not minimize the necessity of the "godly walk," however. Rather, "he is required to sow among his hearers godliness and good works, which latter again are the effects of the Word... but the walk and conversation also of the teacher are required to tend to the same end, 1 Tim. 4, 12: *'be thou an example of the believers, in word, in conversation, in charity, in spirit, in faith, in purity.'*"[44] Here Hunnius echoes Luther's words in the Small Catechism: "But whoever teaches and lives otherwise than as God's Word prescribes, profanes the name of God among us; from this preserve us, Heavenly Father!" (SC The Lord's Prayer, 1st Petition.5)

Before leaving the matter of teaching, Hunnius addresses three questions: (1) "Is it the duty of the minister of the Gospel merely to preach the doctrine of Salvation unto his hearers, or is he also bound occasionally to refer to erroneous doctrines which are maintained, for the purpose of refuting them?", (2) "Whether those who maintain such erroneous doctrines ought to be publicly named in the Church, pointed out as heretics, seducers, false teachers, and publicly condemned as such," and (3) "Are such as are known to live in a state of gross sin, thereby giving public offense, to be publicly punished and otherwise pointed out to the congregation?"[45] Hunnius declares in response to the first question:

> If the Church of Christ were always in such a position as would make it impossible for its members to be misled, it would not appear necessary to refute any existing errors, of which there was nothing to fear. But there are never wanting heresies among us, 1 Cor. 11,19, and every minister is standing in continual dread lest any of his flock be led away from the saving faith.[46]

---

43   ibid., p. 231, ¶ 751.
44   ibid., p. 231-232, ¶ 752.
45   ibid., p. 232-234, ¶ 753, 757, 761.
46   ibid., p. 232, ¶ 753. It is not hard to imagine Hunnius thinking of the enthusiasts, Reformed, and Romanists of Luebeck as he penned these lines.

Thus the pastor has no choice in the matter. Rather, "he is by no means at liberty to be silent ... but on the contrary, bound earnestly to resist the evil, with all his powers."[47] Three proofs are offered for this stance. First, "A minister is desired not only to exhort by the teaching of the word, but also to convince the gainsayers... Tit. 1, 10. ff. ... 2 Tim. 2, 24."[48] Second, "Christ also as well as his Apostles have frequently and earnestly warned their hearers from erroneous teaching, and from those who might mislead them."[49] Third, "Those shepherds that see the wolf coming and yet do not resist, are said to be not the right shepherds, but hirelings, John 10, 12." Hunnius notes in conclusion: "Now erroneous teaching is nothing else than a poison to the soul; and heretics and other seducers are like ferocious wolves; and, accordingly, every minister that is not warning his flock for them is to be considered as a unfaithful shepherd."[50] Hunnius' words might seem shocking in our era of ecumenism and political correctness, but they reveal an area in which we have been sorely lacking. The polemics of the seventeenth century spring from a biblically-based understanding of the pastor's duty as shepherd; here is a bishop who is zealous for those whom he serves as overseer.

Hunnius' response to the second question, whether errorists are to be publicly named in the Church, is probably obvious in light of the above. "We answer in the affirmative; yet it ought to be done, not with ostentation, but in humility."[51] Again, Hunnius offers three reasons for such public exposure. First, we give warnings as the society does around us:

> We do not hesitate to point out publicly the names of those, whose conduct is injurious to Society; such as robbers, felons, etc. in order to warn every one of having

---

47   ibid., p. 232, ¶ 753.
48   ibid., p. 232, ¶ 754.
49   ibid., p. 232, ¶ 755.
50   ibid., p. 233, ¶ 756.
51   ibid., p. 233, ¶ 757.

any communication or intimacy with them.—Thus also in *public schools* the pupil is forewarned by the teacher, in the *household*, the child by the parent, from connections that might do them hurt,—on which occasions the Individuals warned against, must always be mentioned by their real names, without anyone finding fault about it. Why should such not be permitted in the Church?[52]

Second, Hunnius argues (more persuasively) that Christ and His Apostles 'named names' on various occasions. Hunnius' third point expands on the second, observing that Christ and His Apostles "were in the habit of publicly pointing out and condemning heretics." Hunnius offers numerous citations for these two points.

Undoubtedly Hunnius' response to the third question, whether those who are living in gross sin should be named in the Church, is the most controversial of the three. Hunnius' response is blunt: "Public vices ought to be punished publicly, 1 Tim. 5, 20: *Them that sin rebuke before all, that others also may fear.*"[53] Hunnius does say that if the individual is "publicly known"—that is, apparently, readily identifiable as the one whom the pastor is rebuking—then there is "no necessity for mentioning his name..."[54] However, "if this is not the case, then he ought to be named, lest by being passed over in silence, the evil might become greater. But a rebuke of this nature ought to be brought forward with 'all authority,' Tit. 2, 5. that others also might fear."[55] Hunnius' view of the teacher is not for the faint of heart.

However, lest anyone consider Hunnius unduly harsh, consider Martin Chemnitz' words to the city council of Braunschweig upon being offered the Superintendency there:

---

52   ibid., p. 233, ¶ 758.
53   ibid., p. 234, ¶ 761.
54   ibid.
55   ibid.

"But the things that are open sins, these must, in keeping with Paul's teaching, be openly rebuked, whether it concerns a little person or an important one, a person in authority, or an underling."[56]

Hunnius offers a far shorter treatment with regards to the second aspect of the work of the ministry, dispensing the Sacraments. Hunnius defines Sacraments as "holy actions, ordained by God, by the performance of which something real is offered unto, and received by us; by which, as by a seal, the word of God and His promises of mercy are sealed, appropriated, and made sure to us, as also we are made partakers of other spiritual gifts."[57] God's grace comes to us through the Sacraments, for they are the means "by which God appropriates and seales [sic] unto us the promises of God."[58] Hunnius placed an emphasis on the ability of the Sacraments to grant us an assurance of God's grace:

> ...God has always given, as it were, two sorts of assurances, namely, one that could be heard, and a second that could be seen; thus Noah received the word and the rainbow; Abraham had the assurances of the word and the stars, and on another occasion that of the word and circumcision.—In the like manner He assure us, in His word, that His body has been given into death, and His blood shed, for us, and the same thing He assures us of in the Lord's Supper, when He gives us His body to eat, and His blood to drink.[59]

Hunnius observed that as the Sacraments "have been instituted for the glory of God and the wellbeing of mankind," therefore a minister is "bound to dispense the same to all such as stand in need of them, and of whom he knows that they are desirous for eternal salvation, and determined to win the same."[60] However, when the use of the Sacraments "would

56   *The Second Martin*, p. 135.
57   Ec, p. 180.
58   ibid., p. 180, ¶ 611.
59   ibid., p. 181, ¶ 614.
60   Ec, p. 234, ¶ 762.

not tend to the honor of God" or when it would mean the destruction of the one partaking of the Sacrament, then the minister "is entitled *to deny* the dispensing of the same, that he might not 'give that which is holy unto the dogs,' nor 'cast the pearls before swine,' Matth. 7, 6."[61]

Hunnius raised an important aspect of the dispensing of the Sacraments in another chapter, chapter 25, "Of Sacraments in General." Here Hunnius presents the question, "...*whether the ministers of God alone are entitled to the performance of this act*, or *whether such as do not belong to the ministry have also a right to dispense the same?*"[62] Hunnius' is quite firm in his response:

> The dispensing of the Sacraments forms *part of the obligations of the ministry*, as St. Paul writes 'Let a man so account of us as *of the ministers of Christ, and stewards of the mysteries of God..*' 1. Cor. 4, 1. Now as nobody is entitled to intrude himself upon the office of the ministry, unless he be properly called, so nobody is entitled to dispense the Sacrament, unless he be called upon to do so by his office.[63]

The office and the work of the office are not to be divided. Hunnius emphasized this understanding of the divinely instituted office in his rejection of any Donatistic notions: The personal unworthiness of the minister does not draw into question the validity of the Sacrament. Three reasons are given for Hunnius' rejection of Donatism:

> α. In this way the word, if preached by evilminded people would have no effect either. But that this is not the case is proved when we read of Judas, though unsincere, yet having effectually preached the word to the Pharisees and Scribes, Matth. 10, 4. 7, that sat in Moses' seats, Matth. 23, 2.3; ...
>
> β. St. Paul writes Rom. 3, 3: "*Shall man's unbelief make the faith of God without effect?*" The faith of God is accordingly of such a nature as to give us His gifts by means of the

---

61   ibid.
62   ibid., p. 183, ¶ 625.
63   ibid., p. 183-184, ¶ 625.

28

Sacrament; and how could it be possible for the faithlessness of His servant to make this faith of God entirely void.

γ. It is not possible for any one to know the thoughts that animate his fellowmen; or to assure himself of the sentiments that are in the heart of the minister, whilst dispensing to him the Sacrament. As a consequence of this everybody would stand in continual doubt, as to his ever having efficaciously received the Sacrament.—And under such circumstances the Sacrament could not be said to be a seal to the faith of any one.[64]

Hunnius observes one exception to this rule: when "disturbance or persecution ... makes it impossible to get at an ordained clergyman; in which latter emergency such also as are not properly ordained to the office of the ministry are permitted to teach the word, and to dispense the Sacraments."[65] Note, however, this is not a matter of inconvenience— 'emergency' is linked with the impossibility of reaching a pastor, not just the inconvenience of reaching one who has been ordained into the office. Furthermore, Hunnius adds a further restriction to such emergencies:

But yet with this distinction that the Sacrament of Baptism be indispensably necessary, whilst the Sacrament of the Lord's Supper could be possibly dispensed with. In our days the Sacrament of Baptism may happen to be of immediate necessity, but scarcely ever the Sacrament of the Lord's Supper; and we say therefore, that persons who have not been properly ordained to the office of the ministry are permitted to confer Baptism, but not to dispense the Lord's Supper.[66]

This is no idle speculation of an academic theologian—it is the pastoral counsel of a superintendent during the brutality of the Thirty Years War when the Church's enemies sought to suppress her. Hunnius emphasized again in chapter

---

64   ibid., p. 184-5, ¶ 626.
65   ibid., p. 184, ¶ 625.
66   ibid.

XXVI: "God has ordained whom [that?] baptism [is] to be conferred by those men he has called to the ministry of His word. Accordingly He commands: *teach* all nations and *baptize* them. ... If therefore, there happens to be a baptism to be conferred, it must be administered by a properly ordained minister."[67] What, however, is to be believed regarding Baptisms performed by false teachers? Hunnius delineates two categories of false teacher. First, there are "Some that do not keep to the strict command of the Lord, employing for baptism another substance than water; whilst others do not baptize in the name of the Father, the Son and the Holy Ghost, thereby perverting the mode of the institution."[68] Hunnius declares that such ministers have "no right to administer baptism, not because of their being in themselves unfit for this purpose, but because of their perverting Christ's command and ordinance."[69] Undeniably, Hunnius would also denounce those performing such Baptisms today, but what about those who have already received such a 'Baptism'? Are they valid Sacraments? An answer to this question is implied in Hunnius' examination of Baptism performed by the other group of false teachers.

Hunnius observes that there are also heretics who "retain the mode of the baptism entirely unchanged."[70] These false teachers "have a full right to administer the Sacrament of baptism, without depriving the receiver of the benefits this act is able to confer..."[71] Two key points are treated here. First, Hunnius upholds that Baptism's salvific effects are derived from God's promise and Christ's words establishing this Sacrament—not the personal orthodoxy of the pastor. Second, by setting up a contrast between the two heretical Baptisms

---

67   ibid., p. 189, ¶ 640. Please observe that Hunnius limited the direct meaning of the commission in Mt. 28 to the pastoral office.
68   ibid., p. 189-90, ¶ 641.
69   ibid., p. 190, ¶ 641.
70   ibid.
71   ibid.

in such a way as to attribute salvation only to the second case clearly implies that a heretical Baptism which "pervert[s] the mode of the institution," e.g., by not baptizing in the name of the Father, Son and Holy Ghost, *will* "depriv[e] the receiver of the benefits this act is able to confer"—indeed, it is arguably only called a "Baptism" in an improper sense of the term. However, even in the second case, "such people, *who know* this minister to maintain errors, should not go to him, nor bring their children to him for receiving baptism, except in cases of the utmost necessity."[72] However, since Hunnius *does not* counsel lay Baptism in such a situation, it seems that it is still preferable—in his assessment—to receive Baptism from a heretical, but called and ordained, minister than to violate the good order of the Church.

Regarding lay Baptism, Hunnius reiterated the point he had made earlier: as in the case with lay teaching and preaching, so it "is also permitted in the case of baptism being required, if it was impossible to procure a properly ordained minister for the purpose."[73] Two points are offered in the defense of the efficacy of such a Baptism: (1) "The teaching of the word as well as the dispensing of the Sacraments, form alike part of the office of the ministry. As in cases of necessity the exercise of the first is permitted to the laymen, so also must be the latter," and (2) "The Sacraments of the Old Testament have not been administered by the Priests only. Thus we find circumcision nowhere spoken of as one of the peculiar functions of the priestly office. The Passover every man was at liberty to kill and prepare for himself, Exod. 12,6."[74] While the reasoning of the first point seems somewhat circular, the second raises a valuable point. Hunnius recognized a link between the Old and New Testament means of grace—both relying on Christ's merit, with His Sacraments a fulfillment of those of the Old Testament—which eliminates any necessity

72   ibid.
73   ibid., p. 191, ¶ 643.
74   ibid.

to prove the validity of lay Baptism solely on the basis of the New Testament. Because of this relationship, even women may perform Baptism, since "Whatever has been said with regard to laymen, holds also good in the case of women."[75] Regarding the Old Testament, we have "instances of women having conferred circumcision; thus we read of Zipora, the wife of Moses having circumcised her son, Exod. 4, 25."[76] With regard to the New Testament, Phebe and Prisca "have even been permitted to teach in some of the churches; we have also a right to suppose, that they have also administered baptism."[77] Here again we find Hunnius' Old Testament argument much more convincing that his New Testament one; too much must be read into his New Testament example for it to stand alone as proof of his argument.

Hunnius' primary examination of the Lord's Supper (chapter XXVII) spends far less time discussing to whom dispensing the Sacrament is entrusted than is done regarding Baptism. Hunnius allowed no exception to the rule of pastoral administration: "... as the Lord Jesus Christ has ordained His Apostles to be 'stewards of the mysteries of God,' 1 Cor. 4, 1, it is evident that the dispensing of the Sacrament of the Lord's Supper forms part of the duty of the properly ordained ministers of the Church."[78] Unlike Baptism, emergency cannot be cited as an exception to the regular Church order: "... no such cases of urgency can happen, ... no other persons, than such as are ordained ought to be permitted to administer the Lord's Supper. Nor do we anywhere find any command to this purpose, nor any instances of such a deviation from the rule ever having been permitted."[79] In other words, Hunnius maintained that neither Scripture nor tradition allow such a practice.

---

75   ibid., p. 191, ¶ 644.
76   ibid., p. 192, ¶ 644.
77   ibid.
78   ibid., p. 203, ¶ 668.
79   ibid.

Actually, Hunnius spent far more time on the issue of the pastor's self-communion than he did on lay celebration of the Sacrament of the Altar. Hunnius did not even discuss the notion of receiving the Sacrament from a layman; the question is whether a pastor ought *"to go to another clergyman in order to receive the Sacrament from his hand?"*[80] Hunnius declared, "It is most advisable for a minister with regard to the Lord's Supper always to join his Congregation. For in preaching to his flock, does he not also thereby preach to himself? even so in dispensing the Communion, he may dispense the same to himself."[81] As in the questions regarding Baptism, Hunnius appealed to Old Testament precedent:

> 1. *we are nowhere commanded to receive the Sacraments from the hands of others.* For though the Lord Jesus commands us: to *take* and *eat*, it is not necessary to take the elements from the hand of any other man. Thus we do not find that the Manna of old had been put into the hands or the mouths of the children of Israel.[82]

Hunnius also recognized that the celebration today to be participation in the institution, with the pastor standing in the stead of Christ: "It is most probable that the Lord Jesus gave the bread and the wine into the hands of his disciples, who conveyed them to their mouths themselves. Such is also done in our days: for everyone who receives the Sacrament in accordance with the institution of Christ, receives the same, as it were, from the hand of Christ;..."[83] Thus the pastor need not receive the Sacrament from the hand of another clergyman, even when other ministers are assisting in the service: "It is thus accordingly an Adiaphoron, a question of little importance, and one left to the free disposal of every Church."[84]

---

80   ibid., p. 203, ¶ 669.
81   ibid.
82   ibid.
83   ibid., p. 203–204, ¶ 669.
84   ibid., p. 204, ¶ 670.

The necessity of call and ordination to the work of the ministry is maintained by other orthodox fathers. As Martin Chemnitz observed, "And Peter explains himself: All Christians are priests—not that all should function without difference in the ministry of the Word and of the Sacraments, without a special call, but that they should offer spiritual sacrifices. Ro 12:1; Heb 13:15-16."[85] Furthermore,

> ... through laying on of hands the person called is set before God, as it were, so that there might be a public and outward testimony that the call is not only a human matter, but that God Himself calls, sends, and appoints that person for the ministry, though by regular and legitimate means. Moreover, by this solemn act he that is to be ordained is obligated and, as it were, consecrated to Christ for the ministry. Besides, by that rite, as in the sight of God, the church is entrusted to the minister and, on the other hand, the minister to the church, through whose ministry, namely, God wants to teach, exhort, administer the Sacraments, and work effectively in us. ... And thus the act of ordination publicly shows forth the whole doctrine of the call of ministers and sets it, as it were, before [one's] eyes.[86]

Or as Hollaz declares in his *Examen Theologicum* that Lutherans respond to the Anabaptist and Photinian attack on the pastoral office:

> 1. By making a distinction between priests so-called by reason of their ecclesiastical office; and by reason of spiritual sacrifices. All Christians are priests by reason of spiritual sacrifices, such as prayers, praises, alms, mortification of the body; but not all are priests by reason of the public ecclesiastical office. For to women also belong the priesthood with respect to spiritual sacrifices; but not by reason of the ecclesiastical office, 1 Tim. 2:12. 2. Christians are called not only priests, but also kings before God. If, therefore, even when there is no case of necessity, Christians are permitted, on account of their spiritual priesthood, to perform acts belonging to the ecclesiastical priesthood, it follows that

85   *Enchiridion*, p. 29.
86   ibid., p. 36-37.

the same persons, on account of their spiritual kingship, can equally, even when there is no necessity, perform acts pertaining to a political kingdom; from which execrable anarchy would result.[87]

Simply put, Hunnius, Chemnitz and Hollaz say not that any Christian may exercise the office of the ministry (the only restriction being good order), but rather that ministry and priesthood are distinct: if a layman is forced by an emergency to carry out certain aspects of the work of the pastoral office, he does so *as an emergency pastor* (lacking the regular testimony of ordination).

The last work of the ministry treated by Hunnius is jurisdiction, or church discipline. Hunnius noted that "... we have to consider two parties; first that referring to the *teachers*. It is natural that among them, as a body, certain rules and regulations must be maintained (but of this subsequently);— and secondly that of the *hearers*."[88] Hunnius declared regarding the hearers: "These are to be ruled not with wrath and authority, as is done with the disobedient, Luk. 9, 55, 56,— but with spiritual authority. This power the minister derives partly from the *word of God*, Heb. 4, 12—which power we have already had occasion to speak of—and partly also from the exercise of the power *of the keys*, as the ministry of the word is called by the Lord Jesus Christ."[89] Here Hunnius simply echoed the words of the Confessions:

> But we are speaking of the bishop according to the Gospel. And the ancient division of power into 'power of the order' and 'power of jurisdiction' is pleasing to us. Therefore the bishop has the power of the order, *i.e.* the ministry of the Word and Sacraments; he has also the power of jurisdiction,

---

87   cited in "The Doctrine of the Ministry as Taught by the Dogmaticians of the Lutheran Church," by H.E. Jacobs, in *Quarterly Review of the Evangelical Lutheran Church*, October 1874, (4:565-566).

88   Ec, p. 234, ¶ 763.

89   Here Hunnius cites Mt. 16:19, Mt. 18:18, and Jn. 20:22-23 for Scriptural support.

i.e. the authority to excommunicate those guilty of open crimes, and again to absolve them if they are converted and seek absolution." (AP XXVIII.13)[90]

Again:

> The Gospel has assigned to those who preside over churches the command to teach the Gospel, to remit sins, to administer the sacraments, and besides jurisdiction, viz. the command to excommunicate those whose crimes are known, and again of absolving the repenting.
>
> And by the confession of all, even of the adversaries, it is clear that this power by divine right is common to all who preside over churches, whether they be called pastors, or elders, or bishops. (Treatise.60-61)[91]

J. A. Quenstedt (1617-1688) also holds to this understanding of the pastor's use of the keys being one of the chief acts of his office:

> (III) The right and proper use of the power of the keys. The power of the keys is twofold, loosing and binding, Mt 16:19; Jn 20:23. The loosing [power] is that by which the penitent are absolved from sins and heaven is opened to them. The binding [power is] that by which sins are retained to the impenitent and heaven is closed to them. The former is called absolution, the latter excommunication.[92]

Hunnius emphasized that this is a spiritual, not a physical, authority over the flock entrusted to a pastor's care. This, after all, was one of the major Lutheran disagreements with the Roman notion of the use of the keys—attaching civil penalties and bodily punishments to the sentence of excommunication. How does the pastor rightly carry out such church discipline? *"Not by means of worldly compulsion,* such as fire, pain etc., but solely by means of the Word of God; it manifests itself in offering a friendly reception to the obedient and a serious

---

90   Jacobs, p. 297.
91   Jacobs, p. 348-349.
92   *The Holy Ministry*, p. 5.

exclusion to such among the congregation who have no desire to be guided by the Word of God."[93] Such discipline is never done simply "for the gratification of the minister's own inclinations and desires..."[94] However, lest there be any doubt that it is the pastor's responsibility to remove such persons from the congregation, Hunnius added: "Just as a shepherd leads his flock, the obedient among them he is kind to; the disobedient he tries by gentle means to induce to a better course, and if he finds that they are not willing to improve he removes them from his flock, yet without employing more dangerous and hurtful means."[95] Or as Melanchthon put it, "So far we are obliged to obey the minister, and so far has he power and might to command, yet not only to command, for *God* works through him, giving blessedness to the obedient and a curse to the disobedient."[96] If any would challenge Hunnius' assertion of the pastor's responsibility to carry out such actions, he would probably have referred them to the confessional passages cited above. There seems little doubt that this is Hunnius understanding of the pastor's use of the binding key: the exclusion of the impenitent sinner from the congregation. An honest evaluation of Hunnius' text will not lead one to construe this to be a simple 'suspension' from communion, nor does Hunnius bring in any reference to congregational involvement.[97]

93   Ec, p. 235, ¶ 765.
94   ibid.
95   ibid.
96   *Melanchthon on Christian Doctrine*, p. 256.
97   It should be noted that Werner Elert observes, "...the Augsburg Confession counts exclusion 'from the communion of the church' (*e communione ecclesiae*) among the specific functions of the spiritual office (XXVIII; 21; Apology XIV, 13). Basically this was unavoidable after the exercise of the rights given to the whole congregation had been assigned to the spiritual office. ... But as soon as one proceeded to announce the exclusion from the church in a solemn manner— if possible, by using Paul's statements concerning 'handing over to Satan'—there was imposed on him who made the announcement a responsibility which, from a practical point of view, it was impossible for him to bear. It would be bearable for him only if he had been appointed a custodian of morals or rather a judge of morals. This contradicts the Lutheran conception of the office." (*The Structure of*

Indeed, Chemnitz viewed the pastor's ability to carry out such discipline as necessary to his office. As Chemnitz wrote to the Braunschweig city council:

> The council will allow us to carry out our total ministry, not only what pertains to teaching but also what belongs to the area of discipline, be it for false doctrine or ungodly and offensive life. And if for a short time there are misunderstandings and disputes, the council will continue our salaries so that we have the opportunity to clear up our problems with each other.
>
> ...
>
> The honorable council will not hinder church discipline but rather help support it, since the binding key is a necessary part of the ministry. ...
>
> ... if there were no church discipline, I know that the office of the ministry could not be carried out, since the crude mass of the congregation would only laugh at the preacher's efforts at discipline.[98]

C. The Effects of this Ministry.

Hunnius gave further attention to the binding and loosing of sins in the next section—such binding and loosing are the effects of the ministry. The effects of this ministry should not be minimized, for:

> They consist not only in preaching and proclaiming

Lutheranism, trans. by Walter A. Hansen, [St. Louis: Concordia Publishing House, 1962] p. 358-359.) Hunnius would disagree with this remark on several points. First, the appeal to *practicality* over against the proper expression of doctrine must be rejected out of hand. The potential damage caused by such appeals to realistic thinking is such as would eliminate basis for such historic practices as closed communion, the refusal to ordain women, etc. Second, Elert is seriously misconstruing the position of the Confessions and the fathers—the point is *not* that discipline is carried out after the manner of the Reformed, ferreting out every sins, but rather than there is a pastoral responsibility to avoid the damage which the scandal of open sin would do, dishonoring God's name among the heathen, if they were allowed to continue in their sin unchecked.

98   *The Second Martin*, p. 135-136.

of the divine word and judgment, but also in the exercise of a power, something similar to that which worldly governments commit to the subaltern officers and magistrates, and whereby the latter are in duty bound to protect the peaceful subjects and to punish the evildoers. And like as these authorities not only proclaim the will of their superiors, but also, in different ways, do really make use of the power deputed to them,—exactly so has God, which, in our case is the highest authority, deputed to the ministers of Church a like spiritual power.[99]

Quenstedt concurs with Hunnius that this power is not simply an announcement, but actually binds and looses:

...Ministers of the church have the keys of the kingdom of heaven, so that whatever they bind and loose on earth is also bound and loosed in heaven, Mt 16:19; 18:18; that is, they remit and retain sins, Jn 20:23. Therefore they really bind and loose, and they do not only announce what is bound and loosed in heaven. He that has received a key, to loose and to open, he does not indicated what is opened by another, but himself opens. ...

...

... The ecclesiastical ministry [is] not separate from the Holy Spirit but operates by one undivided, divine-human act unto one $\alpha\pi o\tau\epsilon\lambda\epsilon\sigma\mu\alpha$ [official act], not $\alpha\epsilon\rho\gamma o\nu$ [an idle work], but [one] "through which," 1 Co 3:5, not before, or after (or with, only comitative), but as an instrument. For it is one thing that God works conversion by the preaching of the Word and another to work conversion at the same time and together with the preaching of the Word. The former marks the instrumental cause, the latter only the sign or presence of a thing without efficacy. The Holy Spirit is with this ministry with His singular grace, blesses it, and effectively works through it. One may distinguish, but never divide or separate, the outward operation from the inward.[100]

Or as Chemnitz declared:

99   Ec, p. 235, ¶ 766.
100   *The Holy Ministry*, p. 36-37.

39

... But Christ says, Jn 20:21: As the Father has sent Me, so also send I you—namely that you administer the keys of the kingdom of heaven, not according to your will or as it seems good to the world (Jn 6:38; 7:16), but according to the command and will of God (Jn 8:28; 12:49). Therefore, whom God binds in His Word, him the minister of the Word also should bind. ... It therefore remains also for the minister to use, not the loosing, but the binding key against such people.[101]

Hunnius stressed that the penitent sinner "has his sins forgiven him, as soon as he returns unto God,..."[102]— there is not an absolute necessity for priestly absolution first, as the Roman Church taught with regard to mortal sins. Furthermore, the sermon proclaims the forgiveness of sins "to all."[103] Nevertheless, Hunnius affirmed that "There are also in the Church properly instituted authorities, who are entitled to declare unto man (after he has repented of his sins) the forgiveness of his sins—in the same way as, in the case of an individual having been found innocent before a court of justice, he is liberated from his prison by the power which these judges are possessed of."[104] However, three categories of sinners are "unworthy" of such absolution: (1) "Those who have not yet come to a knowledge of their sins," (2) "those who do not abstain from the sins they commit against their better knowledge," and (3) "those who, although they wish to abstain from their sins, yet have not strength to believe that God is willing to forgive them their sins, for the sake and the merits of Christ;..."[105] These three groups must first be drawn to repentance before they may hear the Gospel applied to them.

At this point, Hunnius gave a further explanation of the nature and aim of excommunication. Hunnius emphasizesd

101   *Enchiridion*, p. 135.
102   Ec, p. 235, ¶ 767.
103   ibid., p. 236, ¶ 767.
104   ibid., p. 236, ¶ 769.
105   ibid., p. 236, ¶ 770.

that this action is taken in order that "a sinner might be induced to repent and to seek again acceptance to God. This act is called by Paul 'a delivering unto Satan,' 1 Cor. 5,5; 1. Tim. 1, 20."[106] This action is *not* to be taken against every sinner; Hunnius did not lose sight of the reality of Christian as *simul justus et peccator*, for whom venial sin is a tragic, daily reality. Rather, excommunication is for "those who, after having been frequently admonished to depart from sin, persevere in designedly committing sin."[107] Hunnius is indefinite—deliberately so, in this writer's opinion—regarding precisely how long such admonition should continue. Hunnius perhaps believed this to be a matter of individual pastoral assessment. Several guidelines are clear: no one is to be excommunicated, "unless his sinful ways have before been in *private* and in *public*, pointed out to him, and he be warned against. If he, in spite of this admonition, *is not inclined to repent and mend his ways*, then God's wrath ought to be made known to him, nor should he be promised forgiveness of his sins, but be looked upon as a heathen and Publican."[108]

According to Hunnius, the primary end of excommunication is not punishment. Rather, the aim is "that the stiff-necked might be inclined to come to a knowledge of his evil ways, and repent his sins."[109] This, Hunnius says, was Paul's aim "when he excommunicated the Corinthian, who had sinned in that he married his father's wife, ..."[110] Hunnius also said that excommunication serves the end of "openly censuring sin and its consequences, to induce men in general to abstain from it, and to come to sincere repentance"—citing Paul delivering Hymenaeus and Alexander to Satan.[111]

---

106   ibid., p. 237, ¶ 772.
107   ibid., p. 237, ¶ 773.
108   ibid.
109   ibid., p. 237, ¶ 774.
110   ibid.
111   ibid., p. 238, ¶ 775.

Melanchthon differs somewhat from Hunnius by pointing to excommunication with an emphasis on punishment. As we read in Melanchthon's *Loci communes* (1555): "... [W]e should be obedient to pastors, in their office, if they carry out God's word and exercise punishment accordingly."[112] Again: "I therefore say that as we truly owe God earnest obedience, we are obliged to be obedient to the divine word, as pronounced in the service of the minister, in the sermon, in the punishment of sins, and in the ban. Disobedience is a sin which deserves eternal wrath."[113]

D. By Whom this Office is Administered.

Having treated the questions of the nature of the office and its effect, Hunnius turned to the question of precisely who is to carry out the office of the ministry. Much of Hunnius' treatment of such matters is quite familiar: the office is administered by humans, not angels—specifically, the office is filled by men (whether married or not) who are of "proper age," in good health and who have both the *ability* to exercise the office and *a godly walk and conversation*.

Hunnius did note "that it is not becoming a minister of the word to be occupied, along with it [i.e., the work of the ministry], in any other business."[114] Hunnius does not ignore Paul's work as a tentmaker, "but this is different in our days, since the ministers have to give all their diligence to the study of the word of God, and the addresses they have to make to their people."[115] Hunnius is particularly adamant that "*worldly authorities should not in any way mingle into the administration of this office. ...* But if somebody is lawfully called to the office, and he feels himself fit for it, and is determined to give over

---

112   *Melanchthon on Christian Doctrine*, p. 257.
113   ibid., p. 256.
114   Ec, p. 238, ¶ 776.
115   ibid., p. 238-239, ¶ 776.

his former occupation, then he may assume the office."[116] In general, however, Hunnius is not very enthusiastic about the idea of 'second career' men: "But still it is not advisable to call men of that description to exercise the functions of the holy office, as long as there are men to be found, who have fitted themselves to it from their very youth."[117]

E. The Way in Which the Minister is to Enter upon his Office.

Hunnius emphasized the importance of entering the office of the ministry through the rite of ordination. "Everyone who desires to be a minister of God, ought not to push himself into this office, but ought to be *properly ordained* for this purpose."[118] Three passages are offered in support of this declaration: (1) "I have not sent these prophets, yet they ran. I have not spoken to them, yet they prophesied" (Jer. 23:21 NKJV)—"Thus in the time of Jeremiah the prophets were punished because of their having gone and prophesied without their having been sent," Hunnius observed,[119]—(2) "And no man takes this honor to himself, but he who is called by God, just as Aaron was" (Heb. 5:4 NKJV); and (3) "And how shall they preach unless they are sent?" (Rom. 10:15 NKJV) As we read in AC XIV: "Of Ecclesiastical Order, they teach, that no one should publicly teach in the Church or administer the Sacraments, unless he be regularly called."[120]

However, call must precede ordination. How, then, are ministers called? Hunnius basically skips over an examination of the immediate call, dealing instead with the mediate call. Concerning such mediate calls, "certain persons or classes of the church are entitled to this privilege, viz., the *ministers*,

---

116   ibid., p. 239, ¶ 777.
117   ibid.
118   ibid., p. 240, ¶ 780.
119   ibid.
120   Jacobs, p. 41.

the *authorities* and the *members of the Church.*"[121]   This three-fold responsibility for the call is the consensus of Lutheran Orthodoxy. Thus, for example, consider the words of Martin Chemnitz:

> For the church in each place is called, and is, the whole body embracing under Christ, the Head, all the members of that place. ... Therefore as the call belongs not only to the ministry nor only to the magistrate, so also is it not to be made subject to the mere will [and] whim of the common multitude, for no part, with either one or both [of the others] excluded, is the church.[122]

Hütter wrote: "...the other, a mediate call, such as is now given by the church, which consists of the higher powers or government, the ministers of the church, and the remaining hearers, commonly called the people or laity."[123] Quenstedt also spoke in very similar terms:

> Each part of the church has its functions in calling ministers: [That] of the priests is to examine the candidates of the ministry, to look into their learning and life, to investigate and judge regarding the gifts necessary for the ecclesiastical ministry, and to inaugurate them with the laying on of hands. It belongs to the Christian magistracy to nominate [and] present them and to confirm those that are called and examined. It is the people's [part] to call, to approve with their vote and testimony, [and] to choose.[124]

Hunnius declares that:

The *ministers* are entitled to ordain ministers into the Church, for we read, Titus 1,5: "For this cause I left thee in Crete that thou shouldest set in order the things that are wanting, and ordain elders in every city as I have appointed thee," 2. Tim. 2,2: "the things that thou hast heard of me among many witnesses, the same commit thou to faithful men, who shall

---

121   Ec, p. 241, ¶ 781.
122   *Enchiridion*, p. 34.
123   *Compend of Lutheran Theology*, p. 143.
124   *The Holy Ministry*, p. 17.

be able to teach others also."[125]

Chemnitz also vigorously defended this power of the ministerium:

> As far as the ministerium is concerned, it is necessary that the honorable council will hold to the concept that unity must be preserved within the ministerium, and thus no preacher can be received or called into the conference without the consent of the conference or ministerium, who has not met with and been examined by the conference, and no person may be installed in office without the consent of the superintendent and the ministerium.[126]

Hunnius also defended the role of the civil authorities, citing numerous passages from the Old Testament. Hunnius observes that in those times, "they were bound to take care that the office of the ministry be properly attended to and filled by godly people..."[127] And he noted rather pointedly: "And this obedience has indeed been yielded by all Christians, until the time the Pope thought fit to command them to deny it the higher authorities."[128]

The laity "ought also to have a vote in the election of their minister."[129] The loss of this power, as in the case of the magistrates, was due to papal abuses. "This privilege has moreover been exercised by the laity in the first centuries of the Church, until the Popes took it upon themselves to deprive them of it."[130]

---

125   Ec, p. 241, ¶ 782.
126   *The Second Martin*, p. 136. The hiring of school teachers was even more restricted. "The school teachers must be requested and accepted through the superintendent, so that we do not engage people with fanatical notions or offensive lives for our school teachers or people who are permissive of such things." (p. 137)
127   Ec, p. 241, ¶ 783.
128   ibid.
129   ibid., p. 241, ¶ 784.
130   ibid.

Three steps are given by Hunnius for the process of calling a pastor: (1) the election, (2) the vocation or calling, and (3) ordination. Regarding the election, Hunnius observes: "it is customary to elect a few individuals from every class who as a body are authorized to make this election. —Or in other places it is usual for the lay members of the Church to propose a minister to the other classes, who might either choose from among them persons fit for the office, or otherwise reject them."[131] The key thing here is that it "is left to the option and agreement of the different classes of the Church."[132] When Chemnitz posed the question, "But do Anabaptists do right, who entrust the whole right of calling to the common multitude (which they take the world *ekklesia* to mean), with the ministry and pious magistrate excluded?" Hunnius would respond with the same words given in the *Enchiridion*: "By no means. ... Therefore as the call belongs not only to the ministry nor only to the magistrate, so also is it not to be made subject to the mere will [and] whim of the common multitude, for no part, with either one or both [of the others] excluded, is the church."[133]

Hunnius essentially skipped over any detailed discussion of the call, only observing that the call is the means "whereby the minister is acquainted with the fact of his having been chosen, and requested to accept of the same, and to fill his office with diligence and sobriety."[134] Regarding the third stage, ordination, Hunnius noted that "This is a custom which has been in use in the time of the Apostles, and in the primitive Church."[135] Although there is no "necessity" to this rite, it is retained

> from the free option of the Church,—and because it pleased God to bestow his spiritual gifts more especially by means

---

131   ibid., p. 241, ¶ 785.
132   ibid.
133   *Enchiridion*, p. 34.
134   Ec, p. 242, ¶ 786.
135   ibid.

of laying on of hands, 1 Tim. 4, 14: "Neglect not the gift that is in thee, which was given thee by prophecy, with the laying on of the hands of the presbytery;" 2. Tim. 1, 6: "I put thee in remembrance that thou stir up the gift of God, which is in thee by the putting on of my hands."[136]

F. Different Orders among Ministers.

Although modern Lutherans have come to be suspicious of different orders among the ministers of the one pastoral office, this was not always the case—a fact readily proven from the office of superintendent (bishop) in Hunnius' day, and the continuation of the office of bishop in Scandinavia.[137] Hunnius does not deny that "all who have been ordained by God into the office are fit to exercise its functions to their utmost extent."[138] Nevertheless,

> there are some who, in extraordinary cases, stand in need of advice and instruction, which is not the case of others, who are rather able to govern and to direct. And this is confirmed by our every day experience, that there is among men a diversity of gifts, as is acknowledged by St. Paul himself, 1 Cor. 12, 8. ff.
>
> According to this diversity, God has also ordained a diversity of duties. ... Thus Titus was ordained by Paul to be Bishop (not Apostle) at Crete, and commanded to ordain elders in every city, Titus 1, 5. And experience teaches us that the retaining of the order of things, as described above, has been conducive to the maintenance of order and discipline in the church.[139]

Still, "this order of things we are permitted to change and to arrange as appears most convenient" with the restriction: "Let all things be done decently and in good order, 1 Cor. 14,

136   ibid.
137   "...we have frequently testified in this assembly that it is our greatest wish to maintain Church polity and the grades in the Church, even though they have been made by human authority..." (AC XIV.24, Jacobs, p. 217.)
138   Ec, p. 243, ¶ 789.
139   ibid.

40."[140] What *cannot* be accepted is the subordination of the entire church to one bishop. Four reasons are given for this:

      1. In the recapitulation of the different callings in the Church, 1 Cor. 12, 8. ff.; Ephes. 4, 11 such a common head and Bishop is not mentioned; ...

      2. The Lord Jesus has frequently warned his disciples that none of them should strive to be first and lord over of the rest, Mrk. 9, 34; Matth. 20, 26. 27; Luk. 22, 25. 26...

      3. The Lord Jesus has had, on the occasion of His disciples contending for the precedence, a fit opportunity offered to Him to make known His will on that score. If it had been His will to institute one common head over the Christian world, He would have decidedly done it at that moment. But this He has not done, thereby indicating that He is not minded to have such an order of things in His Church. Finally

      4. Neither the Apostles, nor any of the orthodox teachers have ever assumed such an authority, nor ever endeavored to exercise it.[141]

Indeed, Hunnius says that all the Apostles were given "one and the same instructions, Matth. 28, 19. 20."[142] Peter and his alleged-successors (in the Roman sense) have no primacy in the Church; rather, Hunnius declared, only Christ bears the titles 'head of the Church' and 'chief Shepherd'.[143]

G. The Effects of this Office.

    This section is little more than a recapitulation of what Hunnius has written earlier. Hunnius stresses that the effects of the office reflect the various names given to the office in Scripture (pastor, servant, etc.) This ministry is not in vain, Hunnius proclaims, citing several passages to drive this point home. As Hunnius concludes this very brief section: "And with regard

---

140   ibid., p. 243-244, ¶ 790.
141   ibid., p. 244, ¶ 791.
142   ibid., p. 244, ¶ 792.
143   see Ec, p. 245, ¶ 793.

to all teachers [Paul] says, 2 Cor. 4, 7: 'We have this treasure in earthen vessels, that the excellency of the power may be of God, and not of us,' and, 1 Cor. 1, 21: 'It pleased God by the foolishness of preaching to save them that believe.'"[144]

H. The Means for Maintaining Ministers.

This matter is quite straight forward: "...they are to be maintained by those whom they teach."[145] Hunnius defended this point from both the Old Testament and the New—"they which minister about holy things live of the things of the temple" 1 Cor. 9:13.[146] The case of Paul's tent-making is *not* to be considered a universal: "... yet was it not his intention to have this support withdrawn from other ministers of the word..."[147] After all, as St. Paul wrote:

> For it is written in the Law of Moses: 'Do not muzzle an ox while it is treading out the grain.' Is it about oxen that God is concerned? Surely he says this for us, doesn't he? Yes, this was written for us, because when the plowman plows and the thresher threshes, they ought to do so in the hope of sharing in the harvest. (1 Cor. 9:9-10)

We close this topic with the words of Melanchthon:

> Also let it be further known here that churches and lords are obliged to give the pastors and shepherds of souls their maintenance, as Christ commanded, "To the worker belongs his wage " [*cf.* Lk. 10:7; 1 Tim. 5:18]. What then a pastor saves, or otherwise honorably inherits, or has for himself, his wife, and child, that is his own. And in this case no distinction is to be made between the pastors and other Christian heads of families.
>
> Yet in this evil world pious pastors will probably remain poor, as they always have been. In contrast to them are the godless priests, with their great possessions, who

---

144   ibid., p. 245, ¶ 794.
145   ibid., p. 245, ¶ 795.
146   ibid.
147   ibid.

have imagined themselves in the service of God, as it seems useful for the enhancement of their possessions, pomp and power.[148]

---

148   *On Christian Doctrine*, p. 262.

Chapter XXVIII.

The holy ministry is an office instituted by God in which He has set aside from the rest of men certain persons whose duty it is by His authority to preach His word, to spend the Sacraments, to lead those who are committed to them unto Christ and to build them up unto eternal life.

746. Although God might have been able to teach, direct and govern men without any means whatsoever, yet has it pleased Him to employ certain men for the purpose of carrying out His designs. This arrangement, which has been made for the furtherance of our salvation, we have now to consider more fully. There are especially six points which require our attention: which are;

747. **A.** The names that have been applied to these men; the most frequent amongst them are:

α. *Ministers* (Servants) 1 Cor. 3:5: "Who then is Paul, and who is Apollo, but *ministers* (that is, ministers of God and Christ) by whom ye believed;" Rom. 1:1: "Paul, a *servant* of Jesus Christ;" Gal. 1:10: "If I yet pleased men, I should not be the *servant of God*;" 1 Cor. 4:1: "Let a man so account of us, as of the *ministers* of Christ;" 2 Cor. 6:4: "in all things approving ourselves as the *ministers of God.*" "*Ministers of the Church*," Col. 1:24, 25; "the Church whereof I am *made a minister.*"— "*Minister of the Gospel*," Eph. 3:7: "The Gospel whereof I was made a *minister.*"

β. *Elders*; so called because in the newly planted churches the apostles appointed those to be servants of the word who had either from their age a certain influence over the people, or, what is more probable, who had been longest members of the Church and consequently had more Christian experience than the rest; 1 Tim. 5:17: "*Let the elders that rule well*" etc.; Titus 1:5: "For this cause left I thee in Crete, that thou shouldst set in order the things that are wanting and ordain *elders* in every city."—St. Paul accordingly expresses it as his wish that a bishop should not be a novice, 1 Tim. 3:6, giving it as his reason, "*lest being lifted up with pride he fall into the condemnation of the devil.*"

γ. *Bishops*; which word in the Greek language, from which it is derived, signifies: *an overseer*. Although in the Romish Church this title signifies a very high station in the Church, yet in the scriptural sense, it is intended to denote nothing more than a *teacher* or *minister* of the Christian Church; Acts 20:28: "Take heed therefore ... unto the flock, over which the Holy Ghost has made you *overseers*" (Bishops); Phil. 1:1: "All the saints which are at Philippi, with the *Bishops and Deacons*."

750. δ. *Other names* have been taken from domestic relations, such as: "*stewards* of the mysteries of God," 1 Cor. 4:1; "*labourers* together with God," 1 Cor. 3:6, 9; "*labourers in God's vineyard*," Mt. 20:1; "*labourers in God's harvest*," Mt. 9:38; "Pray ye therefore the Lord of the harvest, that He will send forth labourers into His harvest;" "*fishers*," Mt. 4:19: "Follow Me, and I will make you fishers of men;" *shepherds*, 1 Peter 5:2: "Feed the flock which is among you;" *ambassadors*, 2 Cor. 5:20: "We are ambassadors for Christ."

751. **B**. *The nature of this office*. This office has been instituted in order that by it men might be made fit for eternal salvation. This is done

I. *by teaching*,

II. *by the dispensing of the sacraments*, and

III. *by church discipline*.

I. The *teaching* refers to two things; first to the preaching of the saving faith (for through faith we are saved, Eph. 2:8), and secondly, to a godly and unspotted walk and conversation, lest by an ungodly life on the part of God's minister, faith and salvation might be lost to him for ever. Whosoever desires to plant *faith* into the hearts of his fellowmen must necessarily do two things:

52

1. *He must lay before his hearers the word of God in its purity and uncorrupted.* For faith cometh by hearing, and hearing by the word of God, Rom. 10:17. This word is twofold, viz: the law and the Gospel, Mt. 13:52: "Every scribe which is instructed unto the kingdom of heaven is like unto a man that is an householder, which bringeth forth out of his treasure things *new and old.*" But this has been sufficiently treated of in its proper place.

This doctrine having been properly preached unto the hearers, produces that saving faith, by which they may be justified before God, and made partakers of eternal Salvation.

752. Whosoever undertakes to implant faith unto the heart of men must

2. necessarily maintain a godly walk and conversation. For by this he is required to sow among his hearers godliness and good works, which latter again are the effects of the Word, which is said to be profitable for doctrine, for reproof, for correction, for instruction unto righteousness, 2 Tim. 3:16; but the walk and conversation also of the teacher are required to tend to the same end, 1 Tim. 4:12: *"be thou an example of the believers, in word, in conversation, in charity, in spirit, in faith, in purity."*

753. But as the devil, is always anxious to tear the word of God from our heart, Lk. 8:12, and to sow the weeds of false teaching among the wheat that has been sown, Mt. 13:38-39, it becomes necessary for the minister of the word occasionally to pronounce words of *censure*, exhorting erroneous teachers and other hardened sinners to turn from their evil ways. But this assertion gives rise to two questions, which it our duty to consider.

α. *Is it the duty of the minister of the Gospel merely to preach the doctrine of Salvation unto his hearers, or is he also bound occasionally to refer to erroneous doctrines which are maintained, for the purpose of refuting them?* If the Church of Christ were always in such a position as would make impossible for its members to be misled, it would not appear necessary to refute any existing errors, of which there was nothing to fear. But there are never wanting heresies among us, 1 Cor. 11:19, and every minister is standing in continual dread lest any of his flock be led away from the saving faith. Accordingly, he is by no means at liberty to be silent on that subject, but on the contrary, bound earnestly to resist the evil with all his powers. This we prove as follows:

754. In the first place: A minister is desired not only to exhort by the teaching of the word, but also to convince gainsayers; "There are many unruly and vain talkers and deceivers, whose *mouth must be stopped*," Titus 1:10 ff., "*instruct those who oppose themselves; if God peradventure will give them repentance*," 2 Tim. 2:24.

755. In the second place: Christ also as well as His apostles have frequently and eanestly warned their hearers from erroneous teaching, and from those who might mislead them. Of Christ we know how frequently He has dissuaded men from listening to the Pharisees and Scribes, Mt. 16:6 ff., 23:13 ff.; and how frequently He controverted their views. The same did Paul in his Epistle to the Galatians, Chap. 3:1 ff.; 5:1 ff.; Acts 15:2 ff; as also in that to the church at Corinth, 2 Cor. 11:13 ff.; and the same has been done by pious and godly ministers in all ages of the Church.

756. And thirdly: Those shepherds that see the wolf coming and yet do not resist are said to be not the right shepherds, but hirelings, John 10:12. It is not sufficient for a shepherd to lead his flock on good pastures; he is also required to prevent the wolf from doing mischief, and to keep his flock from straying into pastures that are filled with dangerous herbs and poisonous waters. If he is not considering this to be his duty, then he must be said to be a faithless shepherd. Now erroneous teaching is nothing else than a poison to the soul and heretics and other seducers are like ferocious wolves and, accordingly, every minister that is not warning his flock for them is to be considered as a unfaithful shepherd.

757. β. *Whether those who maintain such erroneous*

doctrines ought to be publicly named to the Church, pointed out as heretics, seducers, false teachers, and publicly condemned as such. We answer in the affirmative, yet it ought to be done, not with ostentation, but in humility. But on this we cannot enter now. That we have a right to mention such individuals by their very names before the Church appears evident from the following reasons:

758. 1. We do not hesitate to point out publicly the names of those, whose conduct is injurious to society; such as robbers, felons etc., in order to warn every one of having any communication or intimacy with them. Thus also in *public schools* the pupil is forewarned by the teacher; in the *household*, the child by the parent, from connections that might do them hurt—on which occasions the individuals warned against must always be mentioned by their real names without any one finding fault about it. Why should such not be permitted in the Church?

759. 2. Christ and His apostles publicly pointed out such individuals, naming them by their very names. Thus Christ named the Pharisees, Scribes and Sadducees, Mt. 16:6: "Take heed, beware of the leaven of the *Pharisees* and *Sadducees;*" Chapt. 23:13: "Wo unto you *Scribes, Pharisees, hypocrites.*" The apostle mentioned by name, as being dangerous: Hymeneus, Philetus, Alexander, 1 Tim. 1:20: the Nicolaitans, Rev. 2:16; Jezebel, ibid. v. 20.

760. 3. Christ and His apostles were in the habit of publicly pointing out and condemning heretics. Thus we find Christ designating the Pharisees as "hypocrites," Mt. 23:13; as "children of hell," v. 15: as "blind leaders of the blind," Mt. 15:14. St. Paul again designates Elimas as "a child of the devil," Acts 13:10;" others as "false apostles, deceitful workers," 2 Cor. 11:13—as ministers of Satan," v. 15.—as "dogs," Phil. 3:2.— That same apostle also *delivered* Hymeneus and Alexander unto Satan, 1 Tim. 1:20; and, accordingly, if such is also done in our days to heretics, etc. (though with humility and great discretion) they ought not to consider themselves in any way

hardly dealt with.

761. γ. *Are such as are known to live in a state of gross sin, thereby giving public offence, to be publicly punished and otherwise pointed out to the congregation?* Public vices ought also to be punished publicly, 1 Tim. 5:20: *Them that sin rebuke before all, that others also may fear."* If such an individual happens to be publicly known, there is, of course no necessity for mentioning his name; if this is not the case, then he ought to be named, lest by being passed over in silence, the evil might become greater. But a rebuke of this nature ought to be brought forward with "all authority," Titus 2:5 that others also might fear.—Thus much with reference to the teaching of the word.

762. II. Another part of the duties of the minister consists in the *dispensing of the Sacraments*. They are to be treated by him as divine mysteries, which have been instituted for the glory of God and the well-being of mankind. He is therefore bound to dispense the same to all such as stand in need of them, and of whom he knows that they are desirous for eternal salvation, and determined to win the same. But in the case of his being convinced that the taking of the Sacrament by any individual would not tend to the honour of God, and to his, the individual's, own destruction,—he is entitled *to deny* the dispensing of the same, that he might not "give that which is holy unto the dogs," nor "cast the pearls before swine," Mt. 7:6.

763. III. *Church discipline*. Concerning this, we have to consider two parties; first that referring to the *teachers*. It is natural that among them, as a body, certain rules and regulations must be maintained, (but of this subsequently)— and secondly that of the *hearers*. These are to be ruled not with wrath and authority, as is done with the disobedient, Lk. 9:55-56,—but with spiritual authority. This power the minister derives partly from the *word of God*, Heb. 4-12—which power we have already had occasion to speak of—and partly also:

764. From the exercise of the power *of the keys*, as the ministry of the word is called by the Lord Jesus Christ, Mt.

16:29: *"I will give unto thee the keys of the kingdom of heaven: and whatsoever thou shalt bind on earth shall be bound in heaven; and whatsoever thou shalt loose on earth, shall be loosed in heaven;"* Mt. 18:18: *"Whatsoever ye shall bind on earth shall be bound in heaven"* etc.; John 20:22-23. "And when He (Jesus) had said this, *He breathed on them and saith unto them 'Receive ye the Holy Ghost; whosesoever sins ye remit, they are remitted unto them; and whosesoever sins ye retain, they are retained.'"* Concerning this we have to consider:

765. *The nature of this power.* This power is not to be exercised over the body, but over the soul; it has not been instituted for the purpose of governing the body, but that thereby the souls of men might be guided and directed.

How this power is to be exercised? We answer: *Not by means of worldly compulsion*, such as fire, pain, etc., but solely by means of the Word of God; it manifests itself in offering a friendly reception to the obedient and a serious exclusion to such among the congregation who have no desire to be guided by the word of God. Just as a shepherd leads his flock; the obedient among them he is kind to, the disobedient he tries by gentle means to induce to a better course, and if he finds that they are not willing to improve, he removes them from his flock, yet without employing more dangerous and hurtful means. And St. Peter admonishes ministers to feed the flock of Christ, not as though they were lords over God's heritage, 1. Epist. 5:3.

Nor is the power of the keys to be exercised for the gratification of the minister's own inclinations and desires, as if it stood in his option to forgive his sins to the one and to the other not. He is bound to do every thing to the glory of God and for the well-being of the souls of his flock—in short, to do everything which Scriptures recommends to this end and to shun everything that might create any obstacle to the desired effect.

Nor is it to be done by *interest* or *affection*, such as love, hatred, influence, presents, etc., all which are at variance with the principles of divine justice, and as even earthly judges are forbidden to be influenced by them, how much less ought this to happen in the case before us?

766. **C.** (cf. §. 747) *The effects of this ministry.* They consist not only in preaching and proclaiming of the divine word and judgment, but also in the exercise of a power, something similar to that which worldly Governments commit to the subaltern officers and magistrates, and whereby the latter are in duty bound to protect the peaceful subjects, and to punish the evildoers. And like as these authorities not only proclaim the will of their superiors, but also in different ways, do really make use of the power deputed to them—exactly so has God, which, in our case is the highest authority, deputed to the ministers of the Church a like spiritual power.

767. With reference to the *forgiving of sins,* we have more especially to consider:

α. that a penitent sinner has his sins forgiven him as soon as he returns unto God, being freed from the effects they would have otherwise had upon him. As, for instance, in the case of the (penitent) Publican, Lk. 18:13, who, as soon as he repented in his heart and had taken refuge in the grace of God, had his sins forgiven him without any delay, at the same moment. Acts 13:39: *"By Him* (Christ) *all that believe are justified* (from sins);" Rom. 4:5: "He that believed on Him that justifieth the ungodly, his faith is counted for righteousness."

768. β. Forgiveness of sins is to be proclaimed to all sinners by the preaching of the Gospel. For the apostleship has been instituted to be a *"ministry of reconciliation,"* 2 Cor. 5:18. The apostles were commanded to preach repentance and remission of sins, Lk. 24:47.

769. γ. There are also in the Church properly instituted authorities, who are entitled to declare unto man (after he has repented his sins) the forgiveness of his sins in the same way as, in the case of an individual having been found innocent before a court of justice, he is liberated from his prison by the power which these judges are possessed of. Thus the Publican

was justified before God, at the moment that he directed his humble prayer unto God, although he had, as is proved by his hastening to the temple, previously repented and found forgiveness of sins. Christ also absolved the woman who had been a sinner, and repenting of her sins, had taken refuge in him, the real mercyseat, although she had previously already repented of her sins, and found grace before God.

770. δ. But we ought to be careful not to pronounce forgiveness of sins to those who are unworthy. As such are to be considered:

a. Those who have not yet come to a knowledge of their sins. Thus the Prophet Nathan did not promise unto David forgiveness of sins, until the latter had declared with a repenting heart: "I have sinned *against the Lord*," 2 Sam. 12:13;

b. those, who do not abstain from the sins they commit against their better knowledge. For we are told that he only is to find mercy "whoso confesseth and forsaketh" his sins Prov. 28:13; and

c. those who, although they wish to abstain from their sins, yet have not strength to believe that God is willing to forgive them their sins for the sake and the merits of Christ; "Woe to the fearful hearts, and faint hands; woe unto him that is faint hearted! for he believeth not; therefore shall he not be offended," Eccl. (Sirach) 2:14-15.

771. Now it is given unto no man to discern the hearts and the minds of others, and accordingly the minister is bound to judge with that Christian charity, which "believeth all things and hopeth all things" and he has therefore to pronounce forgiveness to everyone who properly confesses his sins to him. But he is to do this not without having seriously admonished him, and with the express condition that if what he confesses be true, he ought now by sincere repentance to see repentance by God. To which it would be well to add that God, who knows the heart of man, is sure to punish the hypocrite, and that every thing that is loose in heaven, has been loosed by the office of the ministry.

772. With regard to excommunication we have to observe:

The nature of the same. It is the means whereby impenitent sinners are separated from the Christian congregation, that thereby such a sinner might be induced to repent and to seek again acceptance by God. This act is called by Paul "a delivering unto Satan," 1 Cor. 5:5; 1 Tim. 1:20.

773. *How is it to be used?* It is not to be used as a means against every sinner, but merely against those who, after having been frequently admonished to depart from sin, persevere in designedly committing sin. Concerning such, the Lord Jesus Himself has given us instructions, Mt. 18:15 ff.: *"If thy brother shall trespass against thee, go and tell him his fault between thee and him alone; if he shall hear thee, thou hast gained thy brother. But if he will not hear thee, then take with thee one or two more, that in the mouth of two or three witnesses every word may be established. And if he shall neglect to hear them, tell it unto the Church: but if he neglect to hear the Church, let him be unto thee as a Heathen and a Publican."* Accordingly this excommunication ought not to be pronounced over any sinner unless his sinful ways have before been in *private* and in *public* pointed out to him, and he be warned against. If he, in spite of this admonition, is *not inclined to repent and mend his ways*, then God's wrath ought to be made known to him, nor should he be promised forgiveness of his sins, but be looked upon as a heathen and Publican. Of course, such individuals ought also to be shunned by all godly people, who ought to have no intercourse whatsoever with them.

774. *The end and aim of this excommunication.* The most important amongst them is, that the stiff-necked might be inclined to come to a knowledge of his evil ways and repent his sins. Such was the end Paul had in view when he excommunicated the Corinthian, who had sinned in that he married his father's wife, as he writes 1. Cor. 5, 3ff.: *"I have judged ... concerning him that has so done this deed: In the name of our Lord Jesus Christ, when ye are gathered together, and my spirit,*

with the power of our Lord Jesus Christ, to deliver such a one unto Satan for the destruction of the flesh, that the spirit may be saved in the day of the Lord Jesus Christ." — The excommunication is also designed, by openly censuring sin and its consequences, to induce men in general to abstain from it and to come to sincere repentance. Thus Hymenaeus and Alexander were delivered by the apostle unto Satan, in order "that they might learn not to blaspheme," 1. Tim. 1:20.

775. **D.** We have now to consider by whom this office is to be administered.

α. It is to be administered by *human beings*, not by angels, or any other creatures; more especially it ought to be entrusted to males and not to females. Though the latter are bound to teach their own children, servants, etc. (as Paul writes, Titus 2:3: that "aged women are to be teachers of good things"), yet they are not to allowed to serve in the public ministry, 1 Cor. 14:34: *"Let your women keep silence in the Churches: for it is not permitted unto them to speak; for they are commanded to be under obedience, as also saith the law;"* 1 Tim. 2:12: *"I suffer not a woman to teach."* But an exception of this rule is permitted in case there is an absolute want of godly men for the office, and there are some pious and able women who are fit to be employed in this emergency; as we read of Phebe at Cenchrea, Rom. 16:1, and Tryphena, Tryphosa and Presis (v. 12) having done great service to the cause of the Lord.

Again such as wish to serve in the ministry ought *to have the proper age.* For as little as to that very laborious office children could be admitted, on account of their weakness, even so is it impossible to entrust the same to very old people, because by their infirmity they would be unable to fulfil all the duties of the holy office. Besides this there is no age excluded from the office; not high age, Phil. 9; nor youth, 1 Tim. 4:12: "let no man despise thy youth;" Jer. 1:7: "Say not I am a child: for thou shall go to all that I send thee, and whatsoever I command thee, thou shalt speak." — Another condition of this office is *bodily health*. And if somebody happens to have a defect in his body, he may exercise the office as long as he is not prevented from properly doing his duty; but as soon as he finds it to be an hindrance he had better not undertake it at all. — We have again to remember:

776. β. that it is not becoming a minister of the word to be occupied, along with it, in any other business. It is true that St. Paul whilst officiating in his apostleship continued also his business as tentmaker, Acts 18:8. But this is different in our days, since the ministers have to give all their diligence to the study of the word of God, and the addresses they have to make to their people. As Sirach says, Eccl. 38:24: "The wisdom of the learned men cometh by opportunity of leisure: and he that hath little business shall become wise."

777. But more especially it ought to be remembered, that the *Lord Jesus wills that worldly authorities should not in any way mingle into the administration of this office.* Lk. 22:25-26: *"The kings of the Gentiles exercise lordship over them; and they that exercise authority upon them are called benefactors. But ye shall not be so: but he that is greatest among you let him be as the younger, and he that is chief, as he that doth serve."* Thus we learn from Scripture, that King Usias was struck by palsy, because of his having unlawfully assumed the priestly office, along with his kingly office, 2 Chr. 26:19-20. But if somebody is lawfully called to the office, and he feels himself fit for it, and is determined to give over his former occupation, then he may assume the office. For we know that the Lord Jesus called fishermen, publicans, etc., to the office, Mt. 4:19-21; 9:9. But still it is not advisable to call men of that description to exercise the functions of the holy office as long as there are men to be found who have fitted themselves to it from their very youth.

778. Nor is there any reason for excluding from the office such as are living in a *married state*. For

1. marriage is a lawful state, which has been instituted by God even before the fall of men, Gen. 2:22ff.; and blessed

by Him, Gen. 1:28, — a state which He desires to be kept and considered honourable, Heb. 13:4, and which He has established by a special law; Gen. 20:14. There is therefore no possible reason for a minister of God being forbid to be married; for God does not forbid his ministers to enter marriage, 1 Tim. 3:2-4: "A bishop *must be the husband of one wife, one that ruleth over his own house, having children in subjection in all gravity.*" This injunction we find repeated, Titus 1:6.

2. The apostles themselves are known, during their ministry, to have lived in a married state, as for instance Peter, John and James, 1 Cor. 9:5-6: "Have we not power to lead about a sister, a wife as well as other apostles, and as the brethren of the Lord, as Cephas?"

3. Such a curtailing of the marriage state is expressly declared in Scripture to be a doctrine of devils, 1 Tim. 4:1-3: "In the latter times some shall depart from the faith giving heed to seducing spirits and the *doctrines of devils, forbidding to marry.*"

4. The circumstance that the popes have forbidden the clergy of the Church to marry, has been the cause of the perpetration of a great many vices and other crimes, and the devil could not possibly have had given into his hands a better means for multiplying vice and other offences among man, than just this law.

779. γ. *The qualifications of such who desire to minister the word.* They are twofold; in the first place, the minister must possess a certain *ability* for the exercise of the same. Before he undertakes to teach others, he should first instruct himself; "learn before thou speak," Eccl. (Sirach) 18:19. To which end he is "to seek out the wisdom of all the ancient and be occupied in prophecies," Eccl. (Sirach) 39:1. Thereby he will enable himself to preach the word in a becoming manner and "by sound doctrine both to exhort and to convince the gainsayers," Titus 1:9 and be made, what the apostle calls "apt to teach," 1 Tim, 3:2; 2 Tim, 2:24. A second qualification is *a godly walk and conversation*; whereby the minister is to serve as

an example of the believers, 1 Tim. 4:12. — Now the persons who are admitted to the ministry are not all of a godly walk. Some there are, who although during their ministry they lead a godly life, have yet in their youth loved the world and its pleasures. But this is no reason for their not being admitted into the ministry, after they had been converted and repented of their sins. Nevertheless it would be more profitable to send such to minister in places where their former ways are not known, and thus to avoid offence, "lest he fall into reproach and the snare of the devil," 1 Tim. 3:7. — Others again there are, who, even after their entering their ministry, do continued in their former evil ways; such are not only not fit to be examples for the Church, but they also by their evil deeds, pull down that again, which they might have build up by their teaching. They are therefore not fit for the office of the ministry; inasmuch as, for this, they are required to be "sober of good behaviour, not given to wine" etc. 1 Tim. 3:2-3.

780. E. *In which way is the minister to enter upon his office?*

α. Everyone who desires to be a minister of God ought not to push himself into this office, but ought to be *properly ordained* for this purpose. Thus in the time of Jeremiah the prophets were punished because of their having gone and prophesied without their having been sent, Jer. 23:21. — "No man taketh this honour unto himself, but he that is called of God, as was Aaron," Heb. 5:4; "How shall they preach except they be sent?" Rom. 10:15.

781. β. *How are these ministers to be called?* This is done either without any *outward means*, as was the case with the Prophets: Is. 6:8-9; Jer. 1:15 ff. and as the Lord Jesus called the Apostles, Mt. 4:19-21, etc. — Or certain persons or classes of the Church are entitled to this privilege, viz, the *ministers*, the *authorithies* and the *members of the Church.*

782. The *ministers* are entitled to ordain ministers into the Church, for we read, Titus 1:5: "For this cause I left thee in Crete that thou shouldest set in order the things that are wanting, and ordain elders in every city as I have appointed

thee;" 2 Tim. 2:2: "the things that thou has heard of me among many witnesses, the same commit thou to faithful men, who shall be able to teach others also."

783. The *worldly authorities*. In the times of the Old Testament they were bound to take care that the office of the ministry be properly attended to and filled by godly people; thus for instance, King Salomon, 1 King 2:27-35; Hiskias, 2 Kings 18:4; Josaphat, 2 Chr. 17:6; Josiah, 2 Chr. 35:2; Judas Maccabeus, 1 Macc. 4:42. This circumstance should serve as an example to Christians. And this obedience has indeed been yielded by all Christians, until the time the pope thought fit to command them to deny it the higher authorities.

784. The lay *members* of the Church ought also to have a vote in the election of their minister. Thus we read that Matthias had been elected by the whole assembly of the faithful, Acts 1:23; that the Congregation at Jerusalem had sent Paul and other elders into Antioch, Acts 15:25-26. This privilege had moreover been exercised by the laity in the first centuries of the Church, until the popes took it upon themselves to deprive them of it.

785. For the purpose of carrying into effect the election of the minister in the manner stated above, it is customary to elect a few individuals from every class, who as a body are authorised to make this election. — Or in other places it is usual for the lay members of the Church to propose a minister to the other classes, who might either choose from among them persons fit for the office, or otherwise reject them. But this is left to the option and agreement of the different classes of the Church.

786. γ. *The proceedings relative to the appointing of a minister into the Church.* These are:

1. *The election*; which is a privilege of the parties stated above, and ought to be exercised with a view to the promoting God's glory, the welfare of the Church, and the Salvation of mankind.

2. The *vocation* or *calling*, whereby the minister is

acquainted with the fact of his having been chosen, and requested to accept of the same, and to fill his office with diligence and sobriety.

3. *Ordination.* This is a custom which has been in use in the time of the apostles, and in the primitive Church. The apostles used to ordain the elders by *the laying on of hands*—perhaps for the same reason as the sacrifices of the Old Testament had to be set apart for holy purposes by the laying on of hands, Lev. 3:2; 4:15; or as, under the same dispensation, the Levites had to be ordained to the service of the temple by the laying on of hands, Num. 8:10. This laying on of hand is done, that thereby the minister might know that he has been set aside to be a minister of God's word, and that he might perform the duties of his office with due care and solemnity. And this custom has not been retained from any necessity whatsoever, but from the free option of the Church, and because it has pleased God to bestow his spiritual gifts more especially by means of laying on of hands, 1 Tim. 4:14: "Neglect not the gift that is in thee, which was given thee by prophecy, with the laying on of the hands of the presbytery;" 2 Tim. 1:6: "I put thee in remembrance that thou stir up the gift of God, which is in thee by the putting on of my hands."

787. Thus far we have been treating of the ordinary rules attending the induction of a minister in his office. It is now necessary for us to consider the way in which the great Reformer Dr. MARTIN LUTHER has been called to that holy office, and to inquire, *whether his authority to bring to light again the word of God, and to reform the Church from the errors of popery, has proceeded from God or from man.* We reply: that Luther had been called to perform this great and glorious work by *God,* who did call him partly with and partly without outward means.

788. As the *means,* by which Luther has been called to this great work, are to be considered Luther's having been ordained into the Church, and his having been chosen professor at Wittenberg, where it was his duty to expound the

word of God; as also his having been made Doctor of Divinity, whereby he was bound publicly to teach and to promote the knowledge of the saving faith. Accordingly, as soon as he made it a point to perform his duties in a conscientious manner, he could not fail thereby to bring to light the truth of the Gospel, and expose the errors of darkness. And indeed, Luther has also been distinguished by God, peculiarly in that He blessed in an extraordinary manner his exertions in the fufilment of an office, to which he had been called in a regular way. For it pleased God by Luther's exertions, to cause the Antichrist to be exposed, and to have His word restored again unto men.

Again Luther was called without any outward means. For, in the first place, God has promised to send an Angel, who was to "fly in the midst of heaven, having the everlasting Gospel to preach unto them that dwell on the earth (Rev. 14:6), saying with a loud voice, "fear God and give glory to him... Babylon is fallen, is fallen, that great city and is become the habitation of the devil," Rev. 18:2. Secondly, it is evident that this work of exposing the Antichrist has been a truly godly work, which God has been pleased to have carried into effect by means of Luther. And more especially the fact, that by his exertions the pure saving faith, as taught by the Gospel has been secured to us, against sufficiently proves that his doings have been from God, since none could perform them who has not been sent and inspired by God for this purpose.

789. **F**. *Are there to be different orders amongst the ministers of the Church?* Concerning this question, we have to attend to three different points:

α. that there are to be different orders, because He bestowed upon some men His gifts in a larger extent than upon others. It is true that all, who have been ordained by God into the office, are fit to exercise its functions to their utmost extent. But there are some who, in extraordinary cases, stand in need of advice and instruction, which is not the case with others, who are rather able to govern and to direct. And this is confirmed by our every day's experience; that there is among men a diversity of gifts; as is acknowledged by St. Paul himself, 1 Cor. 12:8 ff.

According to this diversity, God has also ordained a differsity of duties. In the Old Testament there were ordained prophets, priests and highpriests; and in the New Testament, there are apostles, evangelists, elders, pastors and teachers, Eph. 4:11. Thus Titus was ordained by Paul to be Bishop (not Apostle) at Crete, and commanded to ordain elders in every city, Titus 1:5. And experience teaches us that the retaining of the order of things, as described above, has been conducive to the maintainance of order and discipline in the church.

790. β. *But the order of things we are permitted to change and to arrange as appears most convenient*, since there is no certain rule given to us in this respect. But on such occasions the apostoical admonition ought never to be lost sight of: *"Let all things be done decently and in good order*, 1 Cor. 14:40.

791. γ. *In this order of things it is not intended, that the whole affairs of the Church should be put into the hands of, and subordinated to, one Bishop*; for:

1. In the recapitulation of the different callings in the Church, 1 Cor. 12:8. ff.; Eph. 4:11 such a common head and Bishop is not mentioned; for which we conclude, that such an order of things has not been intended by Christ and His apostles.

2. The Lord Jesus has frequently warned his disciples, that none of them should strive to be first and lord over of the rest, Mk. 9:34; Mt. 20:26-27; Lk. 22:25-26: "The kings of the gentiles exercise lordship over them; and they that exercise authority upon them are called benefactors. But ye shall not be so; but he that is greatest among you, let him be as the younger; and he that is chief as he that doeth serve."

3. The Lord Jesus has had, on the occasion of his disciples contending for the precedence, a fit opportunity offered to Him, to make known His will on that score. If it had been His will to institute one common head over the

Christian world, He would have decidedly done it at that moment. But this He has not done, thereby indicating that He is not minded to have such an order of things in His Church. Finally

4. Neither the apostles, nor any of the orthodox teachers have ever assumed such on authority, nor ever endeavoured to exercise it.

792. The Lord Jesus has, on the contrary, given to all Apostles one and the same instructions, Mt. 28:19-20. He has not, for instance, given unto Peter more particular instructions, and adviced the others to subject themselves unto him as their common head. Nor has it ever been His intention that all churches that were to be founded by the different apostles, should subject themselves to Peter and his successors, as their head and ruler. For we know that the apostles never did acknowledge Peter to be their head, but on the contrary Paul writes, 2 Cor. 11:5 and Gal. 2:5, and Gal. 2:11: "I suppose I was not a whit behind the very chiefest of the apostles;" and "I withstood him to the face, because he was to be blamed." Nor do we know of any case that in the primitive Church anyone did presume to take upon himself a position like that of the head of the Church, or who had been considered as such, until the popes endeavoured and succeeded to gain this power of the Church.

793. The Lord Jesus will given unto no other the title and office of "the head of the Church," Eph. 5:22; Col. 1:18; nor that of "chief Shepherd," 1 Pet. 5:4. Accordingly nobody should assume this title and office, which whould be the case, as soon as any man would pretend to be the head of the Church.

794. **G.** *The effects of this office.* These are in a great measure pointed out by the different names which that office bears in Scripture. Thus the ministers are called: "stewards of the mysteries of God," 1 Cor. 4:1; "servants," Rom. 1:1; "ministers" (servants), 15:16; "planters," 1 Cor. 3:6 ff.; "masterbuilders," 1 Cor. 3:10; "pastors," Eph. 4:11; "labourers

in the harvest," Mt. 9:38; "ambassadors," 2 Cor. 5:20.—Now we know that the servants of a house as long as they properly do their duty are not without profit to the household. And in the same way those who have been ordained into the Church, will not labour in vain. The result of the apostles exertions was, as well-known, the propagation of the Gospel of Christ in all the world, 1 Col. 1:23, and that by their means a great number of men have come to the knowledge of the truth. the calling of the Apostle Paul we find described in the following very beautiful words: "I will appear unto thee, delivering thee from the Gentiles, unto whom now I send thee, *to open their eyes, and to turn them from darkness to light, and from the power of Satan unto God, that they may receive forgiveness of sins, and inheritance among them which are sanctified by faith that is in me.*" — And of the office with which Timothy was entrusted, Paul says: "*In doing this thou shalt both save thyself and them that hear thee,*" 1 Tim. 4:16. Again of Peter: "*Who* (Cornelius) *shall tell thee words, whereby thou and thy house shall be saved,*" Acts 11:14. And with regard to all teachers he says, 2 Cor. 4:7: "*We have this treasure in earthen vessels, that the excellency of the power may be of God, and not of us,*" and, 1 Cor. 1:21: "It pleased God by the foolishness of preaching to save them that believe."

795. Finally we have to consider.

H. *The means whereby a minister is to be maintained*; the reply to this is sufficiently clear from the word of God, namely: they are to be maintained by those, whom they teach.

The Priests of the Old Testament had no heritage in Israel, they were to be supported by the tithe, Deut. 14:28-29; by the firstfruit of the harvest, Lev. 23:10; Num. 18:12-13; by the money wherewith the firstborn were to be redeemed, Exod. 22:29-30, etc. For as "they which minister about holy things live of the things of the temple," (1 Cor. 9:13) "even so hath the Lord ordained that they that preach the Gospel, should live of the Gospel," v. 14. It was for this purpose that the Lord Jesus did not wish his disciples to provide themselves for their journey with money and other requisites; "for," says he, "the workman is worthy of his meat," Mt. 10:9-10. And though St. Paul did not avail himself of this injunction, yet was it not his intention to have this support withdrawn from other ministers of the word; for he writes expressly, Gal. 6:6: *"Let him that is taught in the word communicate unto him that teacheth in all good things;"* 1 Cor. 9:7: "Who goeth a warfare any time at his own charges? who planteth a vineyard, and eateth not the fruit thereof? Or who feedeth a flock and eateth not of the milk of the flock? If we have sown unto spiritual things, is it a great thing if we shall reap your carnal things? Do ye not know that they which minister about holy things live of the things of the temple? and they which wait at the altar are partakers with the altar? Even so hath the Lord ordained that they which preach the Gospel should live of the Gospel."

Thus much concerning the office of the ministry, and in general concerning the means, whereby God is pleased to raise up again man from his sinful state, to preserve him in his spiritual life, and finally to make him partaker of everlasting glory.

THE OFFICE OF THE KEYS IN THE
ECCLESIOLOGY OF C.F.W. WALTHER AND
THE LUTHERAN CONFESSIONS

The doctrine of the Church is central to understanding the birth of the Lutheran Church—Missouri Synod and the theology of one of the synod's primary fathers, C.F.W. Walther. Indeed, it was differences between Walther and other Lutherans such as Wilhelm Löhe and J.A.A. Grabau over this article of faith which drove a wedge between their respective followers, dividing the forces of the "Old Lutherans" in this country as they confronted the apparent-confessional indifference of "American Lutherans" such as S.S. Schmucker.

Both friends and enemies of Walther and the Missouri Synod have usually viewed the theologian and his synod as "Repristinators" of traditional Lutheran theology.[1] However, is this assessment accurate? The first portion of this paper will examine a key element of Walther's doctrine of the Church: his belief that Christ has "given the keys of the kingdom of heaven" directly to "[t]he Church...the communion of the saints"[2] and that these saints individually possess the same authority as the pastor, only using it in a different way.

1　Schmucker, for example, could blast "those foreigners in the west of our country, who constitute the Missouri Synod" for clinging to ancient rites such as private confession and absolution which had "long since been abandoned throughout our church in Europe, excepting in that small portion of German churches, known as Old Lutherans..." [in *American Lutheranism Vindicated*, (Baltimore: T. Newton Kurtz, 1856) p. 97.] Walther's friends have been just as strong in their praises, declaring Walther to be an "American Luther."

2　A conflation of parts of Thesis IV and Thesis I of Walther's Theses on the Church, contained in *Moving Frontiers*, ed. Carl S. Meyer, (St. Louis: Concordia Publishing House, 1964) p. 164.

The second portion of this paper will be an examination of the Lutheran Confessions with regard to their teachings concerning the Office of the Keys and the relationship between the keys and the Office of the Ministry and the Priesthood of all Believers.[3]

I.

It seems unlikely that Walther's formulation of the doctrine of the Church would have occurred if not for the fall of Bishop Martin Stephan. Until this crisis, Walther and the other immigrant Saxon pastors were convinced of the necessity of an episcopal structure:

> We have been instructed by you [Stephan] in many things, and from this instruction an abiding conviction has resulted in us that an episcopal form of polity, in accord with the Word of God, with the Old Apostolic Church, and with our Symbolical Writings, is indispensable. Such a form of polity, in which a greater or smaller number of clergymen are subordinated to a bishop in the government of the Church and form a council with him and under his leadership, is therefore our joint, fervent, and earnest desire.[4]

When the little Saxon community was wracked by confusion and a sense of betrayal after Stephan's exclusion they began asking the question, "Are we still part of the Church?" This spiritual struggle resulted in Walther's "Theses on the Church" presented during the Altenburg debate in 1841, and, eventually, in his work known as *Kirche und Amt*.[5]

---

3   H.E. Jacobs' translation of the Book of Concord [*The Book of Concord*, (Philadelphia: General Council Publication Board, 1911)] will be the primary version used in this paper. Tappert's translation will be utilized for those texts not included in the Jacobs edition (e.g. the German text of the Augsburg Confession).

4   quoted from Stephan's Investiture (January 14, 1839), contained in *Moving Frontiers*, p. 134.

5   Given space limitations, our examination will focus primarily on Walther's Theses. *Kirche und Amt*, published in 1852, was the product of a direct request by the 1850 synodical convention that Walther produce such a work. The Milwaukee convention of 1851 "resolved to publish the manuscript 'in our name and as our unanimous confession' [that of the Missouri Synod]." [C.F.W. Walther, *Church and Ministry*, trans. by J.T. Mueller, (St. Louis: Concordia Publishing

Historians have observed that "The theses which Walther defended in this debate [at Altenburg] are basic to all his later writings on Church organization..."[6] The theses are as follows:

Thesis I.

The Church, in the proper sense of the term, is the communion of saints, that is, the sum total of all those who have been called by the Holy Spirit through the Gospel from out of the lost and condemned human race, who truly believe in Christ, and who have been sanctified by this faith and incorporated into Christ.

Thesis II.

To the Church in the proper sense of the term belongs no godless person, no hypocrite, no one who has not been regenerated, no heretic.

Thesis III.

The Church, in the proper sense of the term, is invisible.

Thesis IV.

This true Church of believers and saints it is to which Christ has given the keys of the kingdom of heaven. Therefore this Church is the real and sole holder and bearer of the spiritual, divine, and heavenly blessings, rights, powers, offices, etc., which Christ has gained and which are available in His Church.

Thesis V.

Although the true Church, in the proper sense of the term, is invisible as to its essence, yet its presence is perceivable, its marks being the pure preaching of the Word of God and the administration of the holy Sacraments in accordance with their institution by Christ.

House, 1987) p. 9]
6   Lewis W. Spitz, Sr., *The Life of Dr. C.F. W. Walther*, (St. Louis: Concordia Publishing House, 1961), p. 55.

Thesis VI.

In an improper sense the term "Church," according to Holy Scripture, is applied also to the visible sum total of all who have been called, that is, to all who profess allegiance to the Word of God that is preached and make use of the holy Sacraments. This Church (the universal [catholic] Church) is made up of good and evil persons. Particular divisions of it, namely, the congregations found here and there, in which the Word of God is preached and the holy Sacraments are administered, are called churches (particular churches), for the reason, namely, that in these visible groups the invisible, true Church of the believers, saints, and children of God is concealed, and because no elect persons are to be looked for outside of the group of those who have been called.

Thesis VII.

Even as the visible communions in which the Word and the Sacraments still exist in their essence bear, according to God's Word, the name of churches because of the true invisible Church of the true believers contained in them, so likewise they, because of the true, invisible Church concealed in them, though there be but two or three, possess the power which Christ has given to His entire Church.

Thesis VIII.

While God gathers for Himself a holy Church of the elect in places where the Word of God is not preached in entire purity and the holy Sacraments are not administered altogether in accordance with their institution by Jesus Christ,—provided the Word of God and the sacraments are not utterly denied but essentially remain in those places,—still everyone is obliged, for the sake of his salvation, to flee from all false teachers and to avoid all heterodox churches, or sects and, on the other hand, to profess allegiance, and adhere, to orthodox congregations and their orthodox preachers wherever he finds such.

A. Also in erring, heretical congregations there are children of God; also in them the true Church becomes manifest by means of the remnants of the pure Word of God and the Sacraments that still remain in them.

B. Everyone is obliged, for the sake of his salvation, to flee from all false prophets and to avoid fellowship with heterodox churches, or sects.

C. Every Christian is obliged, for the sake of his salvation, to profess allegiance, and adhere, to orthodox congregations and their orthodox preachers wherever he finds such.

Thesis IX.

The only indispensable requisite for obtaining salvation is fellowship with the invisible Church, to which all those glorious promises that concern the Church were originally given.[7]

A monumental change had occurred in Walther's understanding of the doctrine of the Church. Having espoused an understanding which saw the Church centered on the Office of the Ministry—the episcopal form of polity having been deemed "indispensable"—in 1839, Walther's 1841 theses on the Church never directly mention the *need* for the pastoral office; instead, the only "indispensable requisite" for salvation is "fellowship with the invisible Church," fellowship which is attained by faith in Christ because of the work of the Holy Spirit through the Gospel.[8] "Gospel" is left very nebulous, and we are not directly told that the Holy

---

7   from *Moving Frontiers*, p. 164-165.

8   In his elaboration of Thesis IV in *Kirche und Amt*, Walther does declare, "But if it [the Church] has this command [to preach the Gospel], then thereby it naturally also has the power, even the duty, to ordain ministers of the Gospel." Furthermore, Thesis III of those "Concerning the Holy Ministry or the Pastoral Office" declares, "The ministry is not an arbitrary office but one whose establishment has been commanded to the church and to which the church is ordinarily bound till the end of time." (C.F.W. Walther, *Church and Ministry*, p. 52-53.)

Spirit only works through the means of grace.[9] The Word and Sacraments are mentioned primarily in terms of locating the visible Church.[10]

Having *defined* the 'invisible,' or 'true,' Church in the first three theses, Thesis IV turned to the *power* of this Church: the Office of the Keys. The Church is "the real and sole holder and bearer of the spiritual, divine, and heavenly blessings, rights, powers, offices, etc., which Christ has gained and which are available in His Church." Indeed, we are told in Thesis VII that in "the visible communions in which the Word and the Sacraments still exist in their essence" are only called Church because of the presence of true believers." Indeed, such "visible communions" only "possess the power which Christ has given to His entire Church" because of the presence of true believers. Essentially, it is the presence of believers possessing the Office of the Keys which makes churches part of the "Church" and it is through the presence of such believers that churches possess the power to forgive sins. Because the believers possess the keys, the Church bears "the spiritual, divine, and heavenly blessings"—presumably including the means of grace. The "offices" of the Church are also among the blessings given to the Church.[11]

Essentially, then, Walther's view on the doctrine of the Church is as follows: The Church consists only of true believers.

---

9   However, Walther does state in Thesis VIII that "...God gathers for Himself a holy Church of the elect in places where the Word of God is not preached in entire purity and the holy Sacraments are not administered altogether in accordance with their institution by Jesus Christ,—*provided the Word of God and the sacraments are not utterly denied but essentially remain in those places,...*" (*Moving Frontiers*, p. 165. Italics added.)

10   However, Thesis VIII.A could be read as saying faith is created through the means of grace since it says the Church is made manifest through them.

11   "...the Lord gives to it [the Church] also without fail men who are especially equipped with the necessary gifts for the administration of the ministry, and so He offers them to the church for [its] service." (C.F.W. Walther, *Church and Ministry*, p. 53.)

These true believers are the elect who have been called by the Holy Spirit through the Gospel. As a result of their status as believers, the Church possesses the Office of the Keys directly, and therefore possesses all of Christ's blessings to His Church, including the means of grace and the Office of the Ministry. Of primary importance is fellowship in the invisible Church, which possesses the keys—to this elect number are given the blessings. The blessings are secondary: only the fellowship of faith is "indispensable" to salvation. The "offices," too, must be considered secondary, since Walther writes elsewhere that "when the Smalcald Articles say the keys belong to the church or to the whole church, this does not mean that only entire congregations which have a pastor, possess the keys through him, as a whole [congregation], but even 'two or three', who are gathered in Jesus name, therefore in short, all true believing Christians."[12] Indeed, "all believing Christians, have the command and therefore the right to preach, therefore also have the office originally."[13] To be a pastor means one carries out the functions of the pastoral office: "Even as a person by what he does--what a writer, a porter, a teacher, a song leader etc., must do--becomes a writer, a porter, a teacher, a song leader, etc., so also a person becomes a pastor by doing what a pastor must do... he administers his office, which is what makes a person a pastor."[14] The "offices" are a gift given to the Church, possessing *nothing* which is not given to every

---

12   C.F.W. Walther, *The Congregation's Right to Choose its Pastor*, trans. by Fred Kramer, (Ft. Wayne: The Office of Development, Concordia Theological Seminary, 1987?) p. 25. [From *Der Lutheraner*, Nov. 13, 1860.]

13   ibid., p. 137. [From *Der Lutheraner*, June 25, 1861.] This view is carried over into the *Brief Statement of the Doctrinal Theology of the Missouri Synod* (1930): "Since the Christians are the Church, it is self-evident that they alone *originally* possess the spiritual gifts and rights which Christ has gained for, and given to, His Church. Thus St. Paul reminds all believers: "All things are yours," 1 Cor. 3:21, 22, and Christ Himself commits to all believers the keys of the kingdom of heaven, Matt. 16:13-19, 18:17-20; John 20:22, 23, and commissions all believers to preach the Gospel and to administer the Sacraments, Matt. 28:19, 20; 1 Cor. 11:23-25." (§30)

14   ibid., p. 131. [From *Der Lutheraner*, June 11, 1861.]

individual believer: "Let the papistic Lutherans show that a pastor has something different to do than every Christian is admonished in the Word of God to do, or let them confess that they themselves have no Christian church office. For the fact that pastors exercise the office publicly in behalf of the congregation and the common Christians only privately, proves, as already said, not a different office which pastors and Christians have, but only a different way and manner of exercising the office of the Word, a different use of the same."[15] When Grabau and the Buffalo Synod declared, "Church and teacher of the church are divinely combined, where the one is, the other is to be. They are correlatives; as no bride can be without a bridegroom," Walther shot back, "What do you think, dear reader of this Buffalo teaching?--I probably do not need to tell you what is to be judged concerning it. It is clearly--antichristian! May God preserve our poor church against such a dreadful error."[16]

II.

The 'Whole Church' and the Three Estates. Walther's position having been briefly surveyed, the question remains as to whether this position is consistent with that taken by the Lutheran fathers in the Symbolical Books. For this survey, we will turn primarily to the Augsburg Confession and the Treatise on the Power and Primacy of the Pope. In conclusion, we will briefly examine one example of how these symbols were interpreted during the Age of Orthodoxy (1580-1713).

The Treatise on the Power and Primacy of the Pope provides Walther one of the key passages in the defense of his position. As Walther declared on one occasion, "The chief passages which in the public confessional writings of our orthodox church treat of this [that the keys were given to the whole Church] are found in the appendices of

---

15   ibid., p. 129. [From *Der Lutheraner*, June 11, 1861.]
16   ibid., p. 39. [From *Der Lutheraner*, November 27, 1860.]

the Smalcald Articles, which as a more recent scholar says, was the ultimatum, i.e., the final decision and the letter of renunciation the Lutherans finally gave to the papists after they had rejected the Augsburg Confession and its Apology."[17] These passages are as follows: "...[I]t is necessary to confess that the keys pertain not to the person of a particular man, but to the Church, as many most clear and firm arguments testify. For Christ, speaking concerning the keys (Matt. 18:19), adds: "If two of you shall agree on earth," etc. Therefore He ascribes the keys to the Church principally and immediately; just as also for this reason the Church has principally the right of calling." (§24) The German translation of the Treatise goes on to add:

> For just as the promise of the Gospel belongs certainly and immediately to the entire Church [*der ganzen Kirchen*][18], so the keys belong immediately to the entire Church, because the keys are nothing else than the office whereby this promise is communicated to everyone who desires it, just as it is actually manifest that the Church has the power to ordain ministers of the Church. ... Likewise Christ gives supreme and final jurisdiction to the Church, when He says: "Tell it to the Church." (§24)

Walther goes on to declare concerning the first of these quotations: "These words are of the greatest importance. Every Lutheran Christian ought to know them by heart, especially now, or to find them quickly in his Book of Concord. They are a conclusive proof that the symbolical books of our orthodox church were written under the special providence of God."[19]

---

17   ibid., p. 23. [From *Der Lutheraner*, November 13, 1860.]
18   "ganz, 1. *adj.* whole, entire, undivided, complete, intact, full, total. 2. *adv.* quite, wholly, altogether, entirely, thoroughly, all, perfectly, quite. ..." (Helmut W. Ziefle, *Dictionary of Modern Theological German*, [Grand Rapids: Baker Book House, 1992] 2nd ed., p. 98) From this definition, clearly the intent here is "The Church in its entirety," not "all the component parts of the Church".
19   ibid., p. 25. [From *Der Lutheraner*, November 13, 1860.]

But what do these passages actually say? Is it indeed the same to say "*the Church* possesses the keys immediately" and "*all believing Christians*, have the command and therefore the right to preach, therefore also have the office originally..."[20]? Again, the Confessions declare, "the keys belong immediately to the entire Church, because the keys are nothing else than the office whereby this promise is communicated to everyone who desires it..."—the keys are equated with "the Office". Does this mean that because the Office belongs to "the entire Church" it therefore belongs to every individual Christian?

The private writings of the Lutheran Fathers provide insights into what they meant by the term, "der ganzen Kirchen." The Fathers saw the "entire Church" as consisting of three 'estates': the ministry, the Christian magistracy, and the laity. No part, with the others excluded, was the "entire Church." It is asserted that the passage, "...it is clear that the Church retains the right to elect and ordain ministers" (§72) ascribes to the laity, to the exclusion of the clergy or magistracy, the power to call a man to the Office of the Ministry, but such a view is not in keeping with the views of Philip Melanchthon, the author of the Treatise. Melanchthon restated the ideas of § 72 in his *Loci communes* (1555): "God wants an office and ministry to be in the Church, and he maintains such. Because a ministry is necessary and must be maintained, it follows that the Church has the power and is obliged to choose qualified persons as often as necessary, in the case, if the titled bishops and their supports are persecutors, and will not give to the Church qualified shepherds."[21] However, the reformer went on to make it clear this did *not* mean the laity would be acting alone: "For these reasons which are well grounded and corroborated, the Church shall and must choose and confirm qualified shepherds if the titled bishops and their supporters are persecutors. And from this is it clear that the ordination,

20   ibid., p. 137. [From *Der Lutheraner*, June 25, 1861 .]
21   ed. and trans. by Clyde L. Manschreck, (New York: Oxford University Press, 1965) p. 265.

if it occurs through our churches *and* shepherds, is right and Christian."[22] (Emphasis added) Clearly, Melanchthon was setting forth the validity of presbyterial ordination (as opposed to the Roman Church's insistence on episcopal ordination)— for the laity to call and ordain, to the exclusion of the clergy, would *not* be "right and Christian."

Later Fathers also echoed this understanding of the estates of the Church. Martin Chemnitz (1522-1586), for example, treated this question at length in his *Enchiridion*, which was used for the biannual examination of the clergy under his authority. Chemnitz emphasizes that it is not right when either the ministers or the magistrates exclude the other estates from the calling process, but he also firmly declares: "It is clearly and surely evident from both the commands and the examples of Scripture, that when the ministry is to be entrusted to someone through a mediate call, those who are already in the ministry and profess sound doctrine are to be used. Tts 1:5; 1 Ti 4:14; 2 Ti 2:2; Acts 14:23."[23] Indeed, when he poses the question, "But do Anabaptists do right, who entrust the whole right of calling to the common multitude (which they take the word *ekklesia* to mean), with the ministry and the pious magistrate excluded?" Chemnitz gives the following answer:

> By no means. For the church in each place is called, and is, the whole body embracing under Christ, the Head, all the members of that place. Eph. 4:15-16; 1 Co 12:12-14, 27. Therefore the call belongs not only to the ministry nor only to the magistrate, so also is it not to be made subject to the mere will [and] whim of the common multitude, for no part, with either one or both [of the others] excluded, is the church. But the call should be and remain in the power of the whole church, but with due order observed.[24]

---

22   ibid.

23   *Ministry, Word, and Sacraments, An Enchiridion*, (St. Louis: Concordia Publishing House, 1981) p. 33.

24   ibid., p. 34.

Such an understanding of the entire Church consisting of three estates can be seen in the writings of other Fathers. For example, we read in Leonard Hutter (1563-1616):

> 9. *How manifold is the call to the office of the ministry?*
> Twofold. One an immediate or direct call, as was the call of the prophets and apostles, which was given by God Himself without the employment of any means, and which ceased with the prophets and apostles; the other, a mediate call, such as is now given by the church, which consists of the higher powers or government, the ministers of the church, and the remaining hearers, commonly called the people or laity.[25]

And again, in Nicholaus Hunnius (1585-1643): "781. B. *How are these ministers to be called?* This is done either *without any outward means*, as was the case with the Prophets: Isa. 6:8,9; Jerem. 1:15ff. and as the Lord Jesus called the Apostles, Matth. 4:19,21, etc.—Or certain persons or classes of the church are entitled to this privilege, viz. *the ministers*, the *authorities* and the *members of the Church*."[26]

The view of the Fathers and the confessions, then, seems clear: when one speaks of the "entire Church," one is speaking of the three estates. In light of this understanding, Walther's statement, "when the Smalcald Articles say the keys belong to the church or to the whole church, this does not mean that only entire congregations which have a pastor, possess the keys through him, as a whole [congregation], but even 'two or three', who are gathered in Jesus name, therefore

25   *Compend of Lutheran Theology,* trans. by H.E. Jacobs and G.F. Spieker, (Philadelphia: The Lutheran Book Store, 1868) p. 143. "9. *Quotuplex est vocatio ad Ministerium?* Duplex: Una immediata, qualis erat vocatio Prophetarum et Apostolorum, quae a DEO ipso sine medio facta est, et cum Prophetis et Apostolis desiit: Altera est Mediata, quae hodie fit per Ecclesiam, quae constat ex Magistratu, Ecclesiae ministris, et Auditoribus reliquis, quos vulgo plebem sive Laicos appellitant." *Compenium Locorum Theologicorum,* (Berlin: Verlag Walter de Gruyter & Co., 1961) p. 79.

26   *Epitome credendorum,* trans. by Paul Edward Gottheil, (U.E. Sebald: Nuremberg, 1847) p. 241.

in short, all true believing Christians,"[27] seems imprudent.

But this understanding of the three estates did not begin with Melanchthon and the later Lutheran Fathers—it can be traced to Luther himself. The three estates are apparent in the relationships set forth in the table of duties in the Small Catechism: (1) pastors and hearers, (2) magistrates and subjects, and (3) the household estate. This division of estates certainly played a role in Luther's understanding of the call process. As Luther declared in his lectures on Galatians (1535): "But when the prince or some other magistrate calls me, then, with firm confidence, I can boast against the devil and the enemies of the Gospel that I have been called by the command of God through the voice of a man; for the command of God comes through the mouth of the prince, and this is a genuine call."[28] It is not surprising, therefore, that some Missouri Synod authors have been critical of Luther's views on this matter. The following example is drawn from Mundinger's *Government in the Missouri Synod*:

> ...The first Diet of Speyer, 1526, expedited the control of the Church by the princes [sic] in that it gave each prince the right to arrange religious affairs according to his own desires. It is true, they were not forced to adopt a church polity in which the prince was the *summus episcopus*. They could have adopted constitutions in which the local congregations had much more to say. The fact that they did not must be attributed to Luther. The case of Hesse illustrates the point. Lambert of Avignon had drawn up a constitution for Hesse. In this constitution the local congregation is dominant. In fact, Luther's principle of the priesthood of all believers receives full recognition [sic]. The congregation elects the pastor. There are regularly conducted synods, in which pastors of local congregations discuss their problems

---

27   C.F.W. Walther, *The Congregation's Right to Choose its Pastor*, trans. by Fred Kramer, (Ft. Wayne: The Office of Development, Concordia Theological Seminary, 1987?) p. 25. [From *Der Lutheraner*, Nov. 13, 1860.]
28   in *Luther's Works*, (St. Louis: Concordia Publishing House, 1963), vol. 26, 55 vols., p. 18.

and exchange experiences. ... Philip of Hesse, next to the Elector of Saxony perhaps the most prominent prince in the Protestant Church, was in favor of the constitution and voted thus. Why did Lambert's constitution fail? In January, 1527, Luther suggested to Philip that Lambert's scheme be given up. Philip listened to Luther, and a church polity with the prince as the *summus episcopus* was adopted in its place.[29]

Mundinger adds the bitter lament: "The Great Commoner was not trusting commoners in 1527."[30] Indeed, for Luther had learned the lessons taught by Carlstadt, the Zwickau prophets and the Peasants' War.

The Centrality of the Augsburg Confession to Lutheran Doctrine. The Solid Declaration of the Formula of Concord reminds us that the Smalcald Articles were written as "an explanation of the... Augsburg Confession.... In them the doctrine of the Augsburg Confession is repeated, and some articles are stated at greater length from God's Word,..." (§7)[31] Despite Walther's zeal for the Smalcald Articles, we turn to the Augsburg Confession for our formative view of the relationship between the Office of the Keys, the Office of the Ministry, and the doctrine of the Church.

The Structure of the Augsburg Confession. The ordering of the articles in the first part of the Augsburg Confession, "Chief Articles of Faith,"[32] should not be viewed as haphazard. For our purposes, we will break the first fourteen of these articles in two general groupings: (1) articles one through four, and (2) articles five through fourteen. In the first section, Article I defines Church teaching concerning the doctrine of the Trinity, Article II describes man's alienation from the Triune God, Article III tells us of the Son of God, who reconciled

---

29   (St. Louis: Concordia Publishing House, 1947) p. 15.
30   ibid.
31   Jacobs ed., p. 536.
32   Jacobs ed., p. 37.

"the Father unto us" (§2), and Article IV explains how the Church shares in this reconciliation through faith in Christ's propitiation for our sins.

The second section provides further details regarding how the Church shares in the benefits of Christ's propitiation through Word and Sacrament. Articles five and fourteen make it clear that this participation comes through the work of the Office of the Ministry: "*That we may obtain this faith*, the Office of Teaching the Gospel and administering the Sacraments was instituted (V.1); "Of Ecclesiastical Order, they teach, that no one should publicly teach in the Church or administer the Sacraments, unless he be regularly called." (XIV)[33] Articles VI through XIII are all connected to the work of the Office. Good works spring from the faith which AC V tells us is obtained through the work of the Office (AC VI). Article VII tells us that the Church is located where "the Gospel is rightly taught and the Sacraments rightly administered"—activities only conducted by called ministers (AC XIV). Article VIII reassures believers that "the Sacraments and Word are effectual" (§ 2) means of grace even through the ministry of evil men. Again, Articles IX, X, and XI further explain Lutheran teaching regarding the means of grace administered by the Office. Article XII flows from Article XI, defining the repentance which precedes absolution and reassuring believers of the Church's authority to forgive sins ("the Church ought to impart absolution to those thus returning to repentance" [§2], "The Novatians also are condemned..." [§9]). Article XIII completes the teaching regarding the use of the Sacraments described in the preceding articles, followed by Article XIV which, as was observed above, clearly declares that the means of grace are

---

33   It should be remembered that Article XIV was received by the Roman Church with one understanding: "...that he is rightly called who is called in accordance with the form of law and the ecclesiastical ordinances and decrees hitherto observed everywhere in the Christian world.... Therefore in this sense the confession is received..." [Henry E. Jacobs, *The Book of Concord*, (Philadelphia: The United Lutheran Publication House, 1908) vol. 2, 2 vols., p. 247.]

only administered by those "regularly called" to the Office.

The Power of the Keys in the Augsburg Confession. The Augsburg Confession consistently directs the reader to the Office of the Ministry, not the "priesthood of all believers," for the exercise of the power of the keys. Indeed, the Augsburg Confession only discusses the Office of the Keys in terms of the use of the keys by the Office of the Ministry:

> Our people are taught that they should highly prize the absolution, as being the voice of God, and pro-nounced by His command. The power of the Keys is commended, and we show what great consolation it brings to anxious consciences... (XXV.3-4 Latin)

> ...the Pontiffs, emboldened by the power of the Keys... have also undertaken to transfer the kingdoms of this world,... (XXVIII.2 Latin)

> But this is their ["our teachers"] opinion, that the power of the Keys, or the power of the bishops, according to the Gospel, is a power or commandment of God, to preach the Gospel, to remit and retain sins, and to administer sacraments. (XXVIII.5 Latin)

Indeed, the German text goes on to declare, "This power of keys or of bishops is used and exercised only by teaching and preaching the Word of God and by administering the sacraments"—functions which are only to be performed through the Office. Again, "These things cannot come but by the ministry of the Word and the sacraments. ... Therefore, since the power of the Church grants eternal things, and is exercised only by the ministry of the Word..." (XXVIII.9, 10 Latin). The German text proclaims: "Inasmuch as the power of the church or of bishops bestows eternal gifts and is used and exercised only through the office of preaching..." (XXVIII.10)

Several things can be concluded on the basis of this brief

examination of the Augsburg Confession. First, while Walther locates the Church primarily in terms of invisible priests bearing the Office of the Keys, the Augsburg Confession deals primarily with a visible communion sharing in the means of grace administered by the pastor. Indeed, since we are told: (a) that the Church can be found where the Gospel is rightly preached and the Sacraments rightly administered, and (b) that these functions (preaching and administering the Sacraments) are only performed through the Office of the Ministry, therefore we can conclude that, for the Augsburg Confession, the 'visible Church' is perceived in connection with the orthodox bishop. In essence, where the bishop is rightly carrying out his God-given work, there is the Church. Therefore the Augsburg Confession's teaching echoes the words of Ignatius of Antioch: "Let no man do anything connected with the Church without the bishop. Let that be deemed a proper Eucharist, which is [administered] either by the bishop, or by one to whom he has entrusted it. Wherever the bishop shall appear, there let the multitude [of the people] also be; even as, wherever Jesus Christ is, there is the Catholic Church."[34]

Second, while Walther assigns the Office of the Keys primarily to the invisible priesthood, the Augsburg Confession centers instead on the observation that the power of the keys is the power of the bishops; in fact, "Inasmuch as the power of the church or of bishops bestows eternal gifts and is used and exercised *only* through the office of preaching..." (XXVIII.10 German. Emphasis added)—the power of keys/church/bishops is exercised only through the preaching office ("...allein durch das Predigtamt..."[35]). This does *not* contradict the Treatise's declaration that the keys are originally *given* to the entire Church. The point at issue in the Augsburg Confession

---

34   Epistle of Ignatius to the Smyrnaeans, chapter VIII in The Ante-Nicene Fathers, (Grand Rapids: Wm. B. Eerdmans Publishing Co., 1989) ed. by Alexander Roberts and James Donaldson, vol. 1, p. 89-90.
35   *Die Bekenntnißschriften der evangelisch-lutherischen Kirche*, (Berlin: Weigand und Grieben, 1874) p. 31.

is that the keys are used *through* the Office of the Ministry. Any emergency (lay) use of the keys means that one temporarily serves in the Office—otherwise the clear grammar ("Inasmuch as the power of the church or of bishops bestows eternal gifts and is used and exercised only through the office of preaching") of Article XXVIII must be considered gibberish.[36] As the Treatise says, "Just as in a case of necessity *even* a layman absolves, and *becomes* the minister and pastor of another;..." (§67) In such an emergency, there is no necessity for the usual testimony of ordination.

Conclusion.

With these points in mind, we return to the statements from the Treatise on the Power and Primacy of the Pope which were cited above. Walther had challenged: "Let the papistic Lutherans show that a pastor has something different to do than every Christian is admonished in the Word of God to do, or let them confess that they themselves have no Christian church office."[37] A dispassionate eye toward the Confessions, however, results in a different set of conclusions. For example, we turn again to one of Walther's favorite passages on the doctrine of the Church in the Treatise:

> And in John 20:23: "Whosesover sins ye remit," etc. These words testify that the keys are given alike to all *the apostles*, and that all the apostles are alike sent forth.

---

36   Wilhelm Löhe observes in his explanation to Luther's Small Catechism: "He [Christ] gave the Keys to the whole Congregation, for all the members dwell in His house, and everything is theirs, Keys, Office of the Keys, and Bearers of the Keys, Paul, Apollos, Cephas, all are theirs; given to them for their salvation and blessing and peculiar possession. Yet not all to whom the Keys have been given for a blessing are to bear the *Office* of the Keys, but only the called stewards and servants of Christ. I Cor. iv. I." [*Questions and Answers to the Six Parts of the Small Catechism of Dr. Martin Luther.*, trans. by Edward T. Horn, (Columbia, S.C.: W.J. Duffie, 1893) p. 156.]

37   From *Der Lutheraner*, June 11, 1861, utilized in C.F.W. Walther, *The Congregation's Right to Choose its Pastor*, trans. by Fred Kramer, (Ft. Wayne: The Office of Development, Concordia Theological Seminary, 1987?) p. 129.

In addition to this, it is necessary to confess that the keys pertain not to the person of a particular man, but to the Church, as many most clear and firm arguments testify. For Christ, speaking concerning the keys (Matt. 18:19), adds: "If two or three of you shall agree on earth," etc. Therefore He ascribes the keys to the Church principally and immediately; just as also for this reason the Church has principally the right of calling. (§ 23-24. Italics added.)

Note, then, that the keys are not given to particular persons (individual priests), but to the Church. Furthermore, the point is stressed that the passage specifically references the fact that it is precisely the *apostles* (and, presumably, their theological successors—"the office of the ministry proceeds from the general call of the apostles,..." Tractate §10-German), and not the laity, who are given charge of the *use*, or *administration*, of the means of grace and the Office of the Keys. The amazing unity of many of the key teachers of our Church forbidding laymen to celebrate the Sacrament of the Altar[38] is

---

38   Johann Gerhard: "Es ist allhier ein Unterschied, denn die heilige Taufe ist das *sacramentum initiationis*, dadurch die Kinderlein werden Glieder Christi und Erben des ewigen Lebens, aber das heilige Abendmahl ist nicht ein so gar hochnöthiges Sacrament, daß man ohne dasselbe im Fall der Noth nicht könnte in Glauben zum ewigen Leben erhalten werden, sintemal die geistliche Nießung des Leibes und Blutes Christi, welche absolut zur Seligkeit nöthig, auch ohne die sacramentliche Nießung geschehen kann, dort aber bei den Kinderlein ist kein ander Mittel, dadurch wir sie zu Christo und zum ewigen Leben bringen mögen, als das Sacrament der heiligen Taufe." (*Ausführliche schriftmäßige Erklärung der beiden Artikel von der heiligen Taufe und dem heiligen Abendmahl*, [Berlin: Verlag von Gustav Schlawiß, 1868] p. 22); N. Hunnius: "*a. To whom the dispensing of this Sacrament ought to be entrusted.* We answer that, as the Lord Jesus Christ has ordained His Apostles to be 'the stewards of the mysteries of God,' 1 Cor. 4:1, it is evident that the dispensing of the Sacrament of the Lord's Supper forms part of the duty of the properly ordained ministers of the Church. And as, in the case of this Sacrament, no such cases of urgency can happen, as we have admitted sometimes to come to pass in the case of Baptism, no other persons, than such as are ordained ought to be permitted to administer the Lord's Supper. Nor do we anywhere find any command to this purpose, nor any instances of such a deviation from the rule ever having been permitted." (*Epitome credendorum*, p. 203)

ample testimony to the necessity of maintaining the confessional distinction between these two estates.

One such example of the understanding of the exercising of the Office of the Keys in the Age of Orthodoxy comes to us in Nicholas Hunnius' *Epitome Credendorum*. Hunnius served as superintendent of Eilenburg and as a professor at Wittenberg, only to go on to serve as pastor and superintendent at Lübeck.[39] Hunnius' Epitome Credendorum (1625) is of particular significance because it "became very popular, also among the laity, as a brief and readable summary of the Christian faith."[40] This writer has not come across any evidence that Hunnius' views on the Office were challenged regarding their orthodoxy. Hunnius' work, therefore, is certainly not a bad place to start if we wish to see how theological questions were framed in the minds of his era. Hunnius writes concerning the Office of the Ministry:

> This office has been instituted in order that by it men might be made fit for eternal salvation. This is done
> I. *by teaching.*
> II. *by the dispensing of the sacraments*, and
> III. *by church discipline. ...*
>
> 763. III. *Church discipline. ...* This power the minister derives partly from the *word of God*, Heb. 4, 12. ... and partly also:
> 764. From the exercise of the power *of the keys*, as the ministry of the word is called by the Lord Jesus Christ, Matth. 16, 29 [sic. vs. 19] ... Matth. 18, 18 ... John. 20, 22. 23. ...
> [765.] Just as a shepherd leads his flock; the obedient among them he [the minister] is kind to; the disobedient he tries by gentle means to induce to a better course, and if he finds that they are not willing to improve, he removes them from his flock, yet without employing more dangerous and hurtful means.[41]

39   Robert D. Preus, *The Theology of Post-Reformation Lutheranism*, (St. Louis: Concordia Publishing House, 1970) vol. 1, 2 vols., p. 56.
40   ibid.
41   Nicolaus Hunnius, *Epitome Credendorum*, trans. by Paul Edward Got-

Hunnius' understanding of the Office of the Ministry reflects that of the confessors with regard to the Office of the Keys: the keys are *given* to the entire Church, but they are to be *used* by the Office of the Ministry.[42] When the keys are publicly used by the laity, this means that they are assuming the Office of the Ministry on an emergency basis on that occasion—the regular use belongs "by divine law" (AC XXVIII.21) to those whom the Triune God has placed in the office. To the extent that Walther's understanding of the Church de-emphasizes the means of the grace, the Office of the Ministry and the 'visible' Church, in order to center on the 'invisible' Church which possesses the power of the keys, his construction does not repeat the teaching of the Augsburg Confession in a helpful manner and it risks turning the wavering conscience of the believer away from the objective means of grace which Christ Jesus has established and, instead, directs the individual to look inward for proof he is, in fact, a priest. The efficacy of the means of grace may be construed to rest on the presence of believers (Thesis VII), thus setting up a tautology which may endanger faith: how do I know I'm a Christian? I faithfully participate in the means of grace. But how do I know they are effective means of grace? Because true believers are present and thus, "because of the true, invisible Church concealed in them, ... [visible Churches] possess the power which Christ has given to his entire Church." (Thesis VII) There may be

theil, (Nuremberg: U.E. Sebald, 1847) p. 234-235.

42   Not surprisingly, therefore, the Missourian theory can lead to different conclusions regarding *praxis* than were held by the orthodox Fathers. Whereas Walther says that "...even Paul did not desire to excommunicate the incestuous person at Corinth without the congregation, but he wrote them that, though he himself regarded the sinner as deserving excommunication, the congregation itself ('when you are gathered together') should put away from among themselves that wicked person (1 Cor. 5:4, 13)," Hunnius understands this passage quite differently: "The most important [aim of excommunication] is that the stiffnecked might be inclined to come to a knowledge of his evil ways, and repent his sins. Such was the end Paul had in view when he excommunicated the Corinthian" (p. 237).

a danger of democratic Donatism when the efficacy of the sacraments is even *hinted* at as resting on the faith of believers, rather than on the power of Christ's Institution.

But let it be ever so much an external thing, here stand God's Word and commandment which have instituted, established and confirmed baptism. But that God has instituted and commanded cannot be a vain, useless thing, but must be most precious, though in external appearance it be of less value than a straw. (LC IV.8)

For to be baptized in the name of God is to be baptized not by men, but by God Himself. Therefore, although it is performed by human hands, it is nevertheless God's own work. (LC IV.10)

For even though a Jew should to-day come with evil purpose and wickedness, and we should baptize him in all good faith, we must say that his baptism is nevertheless genuine. For here is the water together with the Word of God, even though he does not receive it as he should, just as those who unworthily partake of the Lord's Supper receive the true sacrament, even though they do not believe. (LC IV.54)

MINISTRY AND THE ORDAINED DIACONATE IN THE 16TH AND 17TH CENTURY LUTHERAN CHURCH

Introduction

The history of the diaconate is a complicated one, to say the least. Although the New Testament contains several references to 'deacons' (e.g. 1 Timothy 3, Philippians 1:1), considerable debate surrounds the precise nature of the role deacons should have in connection with the liturgy and charity of the Church. As one historian noted, "The disappearance of deacons in parts of the institutional church has caused modern Christians to speculate as to whether that office should be restored where it does not exist and what the role of modern deacons should be."[1] The same writer, acknowledging that over the centuries the Church witnessed "the evolution of the diaconate in the growing hierarchical structures," also observed that, "Others, especially Protestants, view this evolution with suspicion and are relieved that the reformation era attempted to return the diaconate to earlier roots."[2] It is not surprising, therefore, that a proposal at the 1998 convention of The Lutheran Church—Missouri Synod (LCMS) entitled "Overture to Establish an Ordained Diaconate" was strongly criticized by some within the synod because the proposed diaconate would be involved primarily in Word and Sacrament ministry, not works of charity,[3] while others embraced the idea of deacons having a liturgical function within the synod.[4]

---

1   Jeannine E. Olson, One Ministry Many Roles—Deacons and Deaconesses through the Centuries, (St. Louis: Concordia Publishing House, 1992) p. 18.
2   ibid., p. 20.
3   e.g., "A Response to an 'Overture to Establish an Ordained Diaconate,'" *Concordia Theological Quarterly*, July 1999, (63:3) p. 205–220.
4   e.g., the Hispanic Institute of Theology at Concordia Seminary, St. Louis, has offered courses entitled "Hermeneutics," "Liturgy I," "Practice in Preaching," "Teaching the Catechism," "Evangelism," and "Administration of the

Given the present debate within the Lutheran Church—
Missouri Synod concerning the office of deacon, it is worth
examining the role of the diaconate throughout Church history, particularly as pertains to the relationship between the
office of the deacon and the office of the holy ministry. Such
an examination should focus primarily in the realm of the
dogmatic theology, while also devoting some attention to the
liturgical expression of the Church's teaching.

Because of the lasting influence of the theologians of
the Lutheran "Age of Orthodoxy" (1580–1713) on the formulation of Lutheran dogmatic theology, writings of that period
are of particular importance when one desires to determine
the historically 'Lutheran' perspective on a particular issue.
Thus, the focus of this paper is intended to be moderate in
scope. The study will begin with an examination of the sym-
bolic documents of the Book of Concord regarding the notion
of grades within the office of the holy ministry and the relationship between such grades and the diaconate. A brief summary of several Lutheran ordination rites will follow this portion, to examine what notion of the diaconate was conveyed
by these rites. Select dogmatic writings of representative late-
Reformation and post-Reformation Lutheran theologians—
specifically Martin Chemnitz (1522-1586), Johann Gerhard
(1582-1637) and Johann Andreas Quenstedt (1617-1688)—will
also be studied regarding their exposition of grades of ministry and the diaconate, to see how the understanding of the
ordained diaconate developed in this later period.

Congregation," to students at the "Diaconal Level." (See Appendix II, p. 16–23 of
Resolutions portion of the workbook of the 2000 Convention of the Texas District,
LCMS.) "Subsequently, 26 men and women have completed the Diaconate Level
program and have been certified for lay ministry." (p. 17)

1. The Book of Concord.

A central aspect of the present debate concerning the diaconate is the question whether deacons should be considered to be within the office of the holy ministry. An examination, therefore, of the confessional Lutheran understanding of grades of ministry is necessary rightly to understand the role deacons may play within the life of the Church; that is, whether "deacon" is one among several grades within the ministry. Modern confusions concerning the notion of grades of ministry are nothing new. As Smith observes:

> A point of confusion throughout the period under discussion (1525–1580) was how broadly one should interpret the office of the *ministerium verbi*. Was it one office, namely that of pastor, so that presbyter and bishop were not different orders? Did it include deacons or the minor orders? Was there a place for elders, such as in the Hesse churches, and were they considered laity or clergy? One cannot answer these questions definitively because of the fluid way in which the various offices come and go from territory to territory.[5]

However, although it is defensible to argue that there was not uniformity on all these points, nevertheless it is possible to speak definitively regarding Lutheran doctrine by examination of the Book of Concord on these issues.

1.1 The Concept of Grades of Office in the Book of Concord.

The concept of grades within the one office of the holy ministry first finds expression in connection with Article XIV of the Augsburg Confession: "Of Ecclesiastical Order, they teach, that no one should publicly teach in the Church or administer the Sacraments, unless he be regularly called."[6] The

5   Ralph F. Smith, Luther, *Ministry, and Ordination Rites in the Early Reformation Church*, (New York: Peter Lang, 1996) p. 3.
6   from the text of *The Book of Concord*, trans. by Henry E. Jacobs, 2 vols., vol. I, (Decatur: The Johann Gerhard Institute, 1996) p. 41. All quotations are

Roman Confutation responded,

> When in the fourteenth article, they confess that no one
> ought to administer in the Church the Word of God and
> the sacraments unless he be rightly called, it ought to be
> understood that he is rightly called who is called in accor-
> dance with the form of law and the ecclesiastical ordinances
> and decrees hitherto observed everywhere in the Christian
> world, and not according to a Jeroboitic call, or a tumult
> or any other irregular intrusion of the people. Aaron was
> not thus called. 2. Therefore in this sense the Confession is
> received; nevertheless, they should be admonished to per-
> severe therein, and to admit in their realms no one either as
> pastor or as preacher unless he be rightly called.[7]

Although the Confutation gives some concern to those who
claim to have entered the ministry as the result of "a tumult or
any other irregular intrusion of the people," arguably the central point of concern was that for a pastor to be rightly called
he must be one "who is called in accordance with the form
of law and the ecclesiastical ordinances and decrees hitherto
observed everywhere in the Christian world," i.e., he must be
ordained by a bishop. From a Roman perspective, *Augustana*
XIV is notably vague on this point. Nevertheless, since the
Lutherans had not yet ordained anyone (with the exception
of Luther's ordination of Georg Rörer as a deacon in 1525),
the Confutation sought clarification on this point: would the
Lutherans receive ordination only from Roman bishops?

Melanchthon's measured response regarding ecclesiastical polity reveals a great deal regarding the Lutheran understanding of the relationship between grades of ministry
within the one office. Article XIV of the Apology replies to the
Confutation as follows:

> The fourteenth article, in which we say that the ad-
> ministration of the sacraments and Word, in the Church,
> ought to be allowed no one unless he be rightly called, they
> receive in such a way as though we nevertheless employ

from the Jacobs edition, unless otherwise noted.

7   Jacobs, vol. II, p. 247.

canonical ordination. Concerning this subject, we have frequently testified in this assembly that <u>it is our greatest wish to maintain Church polity and the grades in the Church, even though they have been made by human authority</u>. For we know that Church discipline was instituted by the Fathers, in the manner laid down in the ancient canons, with a good and useful intention. But the bishops either compel our priests to reject and condemn the kinds of doctrine which we have confessed, or, by a new and unheard-of cruelty, they put to death the poor innocent men. These causes hinder our priests from acknowledging such bishops. Thus <u>the cruelty of the bishops is the reason why that canonical government, which we greatly desired to maintain, is in some places dissolved. ... Furthermore, we wish here again to testify that we will gladly maintain ecclesiastical and canonical order, provided the bishops only cease to rage against our Churches.</u> (§24–25, 28, emphasis added.)

Melanchthon sets forth the difficult position of embracing the canonical polity, while simultaneously explaining Lutheran deviation from submission to that government. The heart of the argument is that the grades, although worthy of retention by the Church, "have been made by human authority"; thus the office of bishop although preferable for church government, is not divinely mandated.[8] Although the Lutherans would normally submit to the bishops, the bishops' rejection of the Lutheran doctrine and oppression of Lutheran candidates for ordination makes it impossible for Lutherans to submit to Roman bishops for ordination. The effect which the violent suppression of faithful pastors could have on polity is reiterated in Apology XXII: "For after the good teachers have been killed, and sound doctrine suppressed, fanatical spirits will rise up whom the adversaries will not be able to restrain, who both will disturb the Church with godless dogmas, and will overthrow the entire ecclesiastical government, which we are very greatly desirous of maintaining." (§43) Thus

8   Edmund Schlink, *Theology of the Lutheran Confessions*, trans. by Paul F. Koehneke and Herbert J. A. Bouman, (Philadelphia: Fortress Press, 1961) p. 250.

Melanchthon turns the Confutation's argument around: by oppressing those pastors who taught the orthodox doctrine, the Roman Church would be to blame if "fanatical spirits" overthrew the canonical polity.

The discussion of grades of office in the Apology is thus seen to be quite moderate in tone. The Lutheran willingness to break with the canonical polity is expressed only in negative terms; that is, that the Lutherans only break with the grades of ministry (despite their origin in human authority) because the Roman party essentially left them no choice. Nevertheless, the Lutherans took the position that there is no divinely-mandated distinction between the grades of bishop and presbyter.

This point—that the distinction between grades within the one office of the ministry is by human authority—is expanded in Philip Melanchthon's appendix to the Smalcald Articles, the Treatise on the Power and Primacy of the Pope. In the second part of the Treatise, "Of the Power and Jurisdiction of Bishops," Melanchthon states,

> The Gospel has assigned to those who preside over churches the command to teach the Gospel, to remit sins, to administer the sacraments, and besides jurisdiction, viz. the command to excommunicate those whose crimes are known, and again of absolving the repenting.
>
> And by the confession of all, even of the adversaries, it is clear that this power by divine right is common to all who preside over churches, whether they be called pastors, or elders, or bishops. And accordingly Jerome openly teaches in the apostolic letters that all who preside over churches are both bishops and elders, and cites from Titus (Tit. 1:5sq.): "For this cause left I thee in Crete, that thou shouldest ordain elders in every city." Then he adds: "A bishop must be the husband of one wife." Likewise Peter and John call themselves elders (1 Pet. 5:1; 2 John 1). And he then adds: "But that afterwards one was chosen to be

placed over the rest," occurred as a remedy for schism, lest each one by attracting to himself might rend the Church of Christ. For at Alexandria, from Mark the evangelist to the bishops Heracles and Dionysius, the elders always elected one from themselves, and placed him in a higher station, whom they called bishop; just as an army would make a commander for itself. The deacons, moreover, may elect from themselves one whom they know to be active, and name him archdeacon. For with the exception of ordination, what does the bishop that the elder does not?

Jerome therefore teaches that it is by human authority that the grades of bishop and elder or pastor are distinct. And the subject itself declares this, because the power is the same as he said above. But one matter afterwards made a distinction between bishops and pastors, viz. ordination, because it was so arranged that one bishop might ordain ministers in a number of churches.

But since by divine authority the grades of bishop and pastor are not diverse, it is manifest that ordination by a pastor in his own church has been appointed by divine law.

Therefore when the regular bishops become enemies of the Church, or are unwilling to administer ordination, the churches retain their own right. (§60–66)

The position which Melanchthon sets forth in the Treatise is the same as that of the Apology, but it is set forth more systematically in the later treatment. The argument of the Treatise is that the presbyterate is primary, with the establishment of the episcopate (in the hierarchical sense) a later human development. Still, for the sake of order in the Church, and to avoid schism, bishops were selected from among the presbyters for the distinctive role of ordination. Because their authority was of human origin, however, when the bishops actually "become enemies of the Church" then the authority which pastors have "by divine law" returns to them.

In light of the understanding of grades of ministry set forth in the Apology and the Treatise, several things become clear: (1) for the Lutherans, the office of the ministry, regardless of the establishment of grades by human authority, is one office; (2) such grades are normally to be upheld, including the delegation of certain responsibilities (e.g., ordination by bishops); and (3) such grades may be ignored when those who have been given greater authority use that authority to persecute faithful ministers.

1.2 The Diaconate in the Book of Concord.

When the topic of grades of ministry are discussed, the Lutheran confessions speak virtually exclusively of the presbyterate and episcopate—the diaconate is only mentioned once (Treatise, §62), and then no explicit statement is made linking the diaconate to the office of the holy ministry. Although Melanchthon cites the example of deacons electing an archdeacon as an argument demonstrating that presbyters are simply elevating one of their own when they consecrate a bishop, it is difficult to prove from this analogy that he is actually contending that deacons are in the ministry. Indeed, the repeated point of comparison throughout Treatise §60 through §66 is between presbyters and bishops. Melanchthon's words in §61 ("...it is clear that this power by divine right is common to all who preside over churches, whether they be called pastors, or elders, or bishops") is, in this context, striking in its omission of deacons. Although it might be argued that Melanchthon, skillful rhetorician that he was, was avoiding further enlarging the debate by bringing up deacons, at this point such an argument is speculative.

In addition to the citation above from the Treatise, the Book of Concord contains two other references to deacons. In *Augustana* XXIII:10–11, we read: "It can be demonstrated from history and from the writings of the Fathers that it was customary for priests *and* deacons to marry in the Christian church of former times. Paul therefore said in 1 Tim. 3:2, 'A bishop must be above reproach, married only once." It is worth noting that Melanchthon applies Paul's words in 1 Tim. 3 to priests and deacons, but this may simply be an argument from the greater to the lesser—if bishops are not forbidden to marry, why should a deacon be forbidden the same right? However one wishes to interpret the passage in this context, clearly Melanchthon did not intend a defense of the diaconate being one office with the presbyterate.

Again, in *Augustana* XXIV:37–38, the confessors declare, "The ancient canons also indicate that one man officiated and communicated the other priests and deacons, for the words of the Nicene canon read, 'After the priests the deacons shall receive the sacrament in order from the bishop or priest.'" As this passage shows deacons as recipients of the Sacrament, and not as those who consecrate or distribute it, it is difficult to imagine this passage providing support for the position that deacons are simply a grade of ministry, such as presbyters and bishops.

In conclusion, therefore, the Lutheran confessions clearly set forth the understanding that the one office of the holy ministry may be divided, by human authority, into various grades, such as bishops and presbyters. However, there is no clear statement in the Book of Concord establishing deacons as such a grade of minister.

2. Ordination Rites of Lutheran Deacons in the Reformation Era.

As was observed above in 1.1, prior to the Diet of Augsburg, the Lutherans appear to have carefully avoided ordaining anyone to the presbyterate. However, one notable ordination did occur in 1525:

> Less than a year later Luther performed what is believed to be the first evangelical ordination of record

when he made Georg Rörer a deacon on May 14, 1525. There is no record concerning the rite except that it took place in the city church of Wittenberg, before the gathered community, with prayer and laying on of hands. But this was the only such liturgical act of evangelical ordination in the 1520's of record.[9]

Certainly, the fact that the first Lutheran ordination (occurring within the period of Luther's 1523–1525 liturgical reforms in Wittenberg) was to the diaconate is not insignificant to the question whether there is a role for ordained deacons within the Lutheran Church.[10] Still, it appears that this ordination was an isolated incident.

2.1 The Homberg Church Order (1526).

Despite the fact that no further ordinations are known to have occurred before the Diet of Augsburg, this did not stop the reformers from exploring possible future rites, and, in at least one case, from including an ordination rite in a church order. The 1526 Homberg Church Order of Hesse included an ordination rite which read, in part, as follows:

> While the bishop, or the visitors, or the thirteen electors, or the assistants of the bishop [deacons] are being ordained, one of those laying on hands should say, "Receive the Holy Spirit." And while hands are being placed on the others one of them should say: "May the Lord fill you with his Spirit, may the Lord teach your heart, and strengthen it with faith, so that you might worthily fulfill the ministry to which you have been elected. Response: Amen.[11]

The lack of discrimination between bishops and deacons is

---

9   Smith, p. 62.

10   Rörer is best known for his significant contributions to the German translation of the Old Testament, as well as for his work editing Luther's letters and other writings. *The Lutheran Cyclopedia*, ed. by H. E. Jacobs and John A. W. Haas, (New York: Charles Scribner's Sons, 1899) p. 413.

11   cited in Smith, p. 90.

quite striking: hands are laid on both, and both receive the same blessing upon them. Certainly this rite would have left the congregation and participants with the distinct impression there was no essential difference of office. Thus Smith rightly observes:

> On the basis of the structure and content of this brief rite [Homberg 1526] one can conclude that the ordination was to the ministry of the word in the interest of the *utilitas ecclesiae*. Leading a holy and upright life was central to election to office: "No bishop or deacon may be admitted or confirmed unless they will teach the word purely and live the life worthy of ministers of Christ and of the church." The recurring reference in the Order to bishop and deacon, no use of the word presbyter or priest, reveal the concern to abandon almost all the minor and major orders and their accompanying distinctions of status.[12]

The reference to both bishops and deacons as those who must "teach the word purely and live a life worthy of ministers of Christ and of the church" makes it clear that the authors of the Homberg rite present both grades as part of the same ministry. Although the relative levels of responsibility might vary greatly between a bishop and a deacon, both were understood to be teachers of the Church and both would be examined to see whether they were able to fulfill their calling—to see whether they were "apt to teach."

2.2 The Braunschweig Church Order (1528).

However, one can also find examples of "Protestant" deacons (i.e., distributors of charity) in pre-Augsburg church orders. For Example, Olson reports of the 1528 Braunschweig Church Order:

> In the church order for Braunschweig (1528), his [Bugenhagen's] first and an example for the rest, there were at least two differences from Wittenberg: (1) the people who were doing the work of deacons were called deacons, and

12   ibid., p. 91. (The word "Deacons" is bracketed in Smith's translation.)

(2) there were two common chests recommended for large parishes rather than one: a poor chest for the those [sic] in need and a church chest for church supplies and repairs; salaries of preachers, sacristans, and organists; and housing for preachers and schoolmasters. Deacons chosen by the council and members of the commune were in charge of the chests. There were to be three deacons for the poor chest, and four for the church chest. Both sets of deacons were similar in their responsibilities for money, record-keeping, and accountability to an "Honorable Council" and the "Ten Men," but they differed in that the four deacons of the church chest had "authority from the commune in company with the council to appoint a preacher."[13]

The Braunschweig deacons reflect, therefore, a markedly different understanding of the office of deacon than is reflected in the Homberg order. Given Johannes Bugenhagen's critical role in formulating many of the early Lutheran church orders, one might be tempted to give great weight to this concept of the diaconate. However, apparently very little is known concerning the implementation of such notions outside of Braunschweig; as Olson concedes: "Scholars have not determined whether his ideas were put into effect wherever he worked. Much work remains to be done, not only in the cities and territories where Bugenhagen worked, but elsewhere as well."[14] Indeed, Olson offers no later examples of "Protestant" deacons in the Reformation-era Lutheran Church. Although she does seek support from Luther's writings, the vast majority of Olson's citations endorsing the understanding of deacons being involved in charity, not the office of preaching, date from before 1523. The only later example Olson offers from Luther comes from a 1528 lecture where he observed:

There were deacons who also at one time preached. From Acts: *they established seven*, who presided over the church in providing for the poor and widows. These deacons sometimes also preached, e.g., Stephen, and were admitted

13   Olson, p. 105.
14   ibid., p. 107.

to other offices of the church although the chief task was to provide for the poor and widows. ...

... There ought to be deacons of the church who ought to serve the bishop and to rule the church in external things according to his counsel.[15]

2.3 John Frederick's 1535 Decree and Luther's Ordination Rite of 1539.

With the Homberg and Braunschweig Church Orders, one is presented with two quite different concepts regarding the diaconate. Again, it should be remembered that the Homberg 1526 rite was not used before the Diet of Augsburg in 1530. Even after Augsburg, however, it was still several years before there was a move toward establishing a uniform practice for ordination. Finally, in 1535, the elector of Saxony moved to establish a degree of regularity to ordinations:

> So Elector John Frederick issued a decree in 1535 centralizing ordinations in Wittenberg. No extant copy of the decree itself exists but we know its content on the basis of instructions of the Elector to the visitors of Meissen and Vogtland, dated May 12, 1535, Torgau. They were to inform the superintendents that henceforth everyone who desired an office in the electorate should be examined by the superintendent and then sent, with a letter of attestation, to the faculty at Wittenberg to whom the Elector had given the mandate "to ordain and thus to give the power and authority of the office of priest and deacon."[16]

John Frederick's decree certainly reinforced the ordained diaconate by establishing that the superintendent had authority to ordain them. Moreover, the decree made it clear that such ordination was not an indifferent rite; rather, the decree explicitly declared, "You know that the ordination of the church with its rite is necessary."[17] The elector's assessment of the

---

15   ibid., p. 99–11.
16   Smith, p. 66.
17   ibid., p. 67.

importance of ordination calls to mind Melanchthon's words from Article XIII of the Apology of the Augsburg Confession:

> But if ordination be understood as applying to the ministry of the Word, we will not be unwilling to call ordination a sacrament. For the ministry of the Word has God's command and glorious promises (Rom. 1:16): "The Gospel is the power of God unto salvation to every one that believeth." Likewise, (Isa. 55:11): "So shall my word be that goeth forth out of my mouth; it shall not return unto me void, but it shall accomplish that which I please." If ordination be understood in this way, neither will we refuse to call the imposition of hands a sacrament. For the Church has the command to appoint ministers, which should be most pleasing to us, because we know that God approves this ministry, and is present in the ministry. And it is of advantage, so far as can be done, to adorn the ministry of the Word with every kind of praise against fanatical men, who dream that the Holy Ghost is given not through the Word, but because of certain preparations of their own... (§11–13)

Given the Apology's status (together with the *Augustana*) as a public confession of Lutheran doctrine, John Frederick's proclamation of 1535 should be read in light of Melanchthon's words in the Apology. One must therefore take John Frederick's decree regarding the ordination of priests and deacons very seriously. If Reformation-era Lutherans valued ordination so highly as to rank it as a "sacrament," certainly John Frederick's instructions regarding the ordination of deacons cannot be seen as an empty rite, but was intended to convey that "God approves this ministry, and is present in the ministry." (§12)

Beginning in 1535, Johannes Bugenhagen was chosen as general superintendent and city pastor of Wittenberg, and thus ordinator for the city, despite Bugenhagen's contention (*contra* Luther) that ordinations should occur "in the community by which the person had been called."[18] However, despite the establishment of a formal structure for ordinations, the Lutherans were still slow to begin to ordain candidates: the first official Wittenberg ordination occurred on July 29, 1537.[19] Given Bugenhagen's opposition to centralized ordinations, it is perhaps not too surprising that ordinations did not become a regular event in Wittenberg until after Bugenhagen left for Denmark in 1537. With Luther assuming responsibility as ordinator, ordinations began occurring regularly and he composed a new ordination rite in 1539.

Luther's rite makes it implicitly clear that bishops and presbyters share the same office, referring 1 Tim. 3:1–7 to presbyters. Luther gives the instruction, "The ordinator addresses the ordinands in these or similar words: Herein you hear that *we bishops—i.e., presbyters and pastors*—are called not to watch over geese or cows, but over the congregation God purchased with his own blood that we should feed them with the pure Word of God and also be on guard lest wolves and sects burst in among the poor sheep."[20] (Emph. added) Again, given the Lutheran understanding of grades of ministry, the equivalence between bishops and presbyters is not surprising. However, deacons are not mentioned in the rite, so no clear inference regarding their status can be made from this rite, except as an argument from silence. Still, in summarizing Luther's ordination rites, Smith observes:

> One must note also that Luther's use of the liturgical act of ordaining indicated his conviction that there was but one office of the *ministerium verbi*. To be sure, there could be different roles played out within that one office, but the liturgical action revealed an inherent equality among the pastor of a congregation (the 1535/39), the bishop overseeing many congregations (the 1542 episcopal ordination), and

---

18   ibid., p. 68–69.
19   ibid., p. 71.
20   Martin Luther, "Ordination of Ministers of the Word," *Luther's Works*, 55 vols., vol 53 (Philadelphia: Fortress Press, 1965)p. 125.

the deacon assisting in the life of the community (the 1525 ordination of Rörer). The focus in all cases was on the fact that through this liturgical act one was ordained into an office which served the whole church.[21]

Despite Luther's early writings favoring a diaconate concerned with the charity of the Church, John Frederick's decree regarding ordination for priests and deacons, Luther's ordination of Rörer, and the Homberg rite demonstrate that the notion of the diaconate as a grade of ministry was a defensible position in the years immediately preceding and following the Diet of Augsburg.

2.4 The Würtemberg Rites of 1547 and 1559.

The Würtemberg rites of 1547 and 1559 also reinforced the concept of deacons as a grade within the office of the ministry. The 1547 *Synodalordnung* specifically stated that "The Dean of the area was in charge of the 'ordination' of new pastors and deacons."[22] And a prayer concerning the "worthy office of preaching" was prayed over deacons and pastors alike:

Almighty God, Heavenly Father you have instituted the worthy office of preaching through your beloved Son, Jesus Christ, so that poor humanity might be comforted and helped. You have also stated and promised that those who believe and are baptized will be blessed. Because we know that our corrupt and awful flesh is troublesome and dangerous, we pray your special help and gracious assistance to protect this dear and worthy treasure from the greatly depraved and wrathful enemy, which we would not be capable of doing in our miserable, weak, and earthly vessels. We ask you in your boundless grace and mercy, that you would not leave or abandon us, but would hold us in your divine hand. We especially pray for your servant, N., who has been sworn to preach the Holy Gospel, that he may remain steadfast against all onslaughts of the Devil,

---

21   Smith, p. 161.
22   ibid., p. 164.

steadfast in your healing, useful and necessary command until the end of the earth in your sacred kingdom. We pray that we may never be deprived of your heavenly comfort, through Jesus Christ your Son, our Lord, who with you and the Holy Spirit lives and reigns, one God forever. Amen.[23] (Emph. added.)

Clearly the Würtemberg rite set forth the expectation that deacons would preach, and were in the "worthy office." Thus the diaconate was clearly understood to be a grade of ministry. Lest there be any doubt regarding this point, it is worth noting that when the ordinator placed his right hand on the head of the new pastor or deacon (the same words were used at the ordination of both pastors and deacons), he declared:

> Dear brother, we have gathered in the Holy Spirit, have called out and prayed to God our Heavenly Father through Jesus Christ our Lord and Savior on your account. We do not doubt that He has heard us according to His divine promise, and that He will grant our petitions. Accordingly, by command of the Almighty and by command of our gracious Prince and Lord, who is the right and God-given magistrate, I ordain, confirm and certify you as servant and pastor of this congregation. All of this with the earnest command that you would energetically and faithfully administer this with all honesty and without anger, as you must give account on that day before the judgment seat of our Lord Jesus Christ, the true judge, in the name of the Father and of the Son and of the Holy Spirit. Amen.[24] (Emph. added.)

Although a man may be called to serve as deacon, his ordination (in the Würtemberg rite) left no doubt that he had been ordained into the ministry of Word and Sacrament. Both the ordination prayer and the blessing made it clear that both pastors and deacons act as "servant and pastor"; both are "sworn to preach the holy Gospel." Unlike the Homberg

---

23   ibid., p. 165.
24   ibid., p. 166.

and Braunschweig rites, the Würtemberg rite is not easily attributable to the fluctuating character of the first decade of the Reformation; it is far more difficult to postulate that the Würtembergers were 'experimenting' as sometimes occurred in the heady days of the early of the Reformation (e.g., Carlstadt's reforms at Wittenberg during Luther's exile at the Wartburg). Furthermore, when the Würtemberg Church Order was revised in 1559, the understanding of the diaconate as a grade of ministry was not withdrawn, but expanded: "Only presbyters and deacons were discussed in this 1547 Order, although the role of a 'Superintendent' was mentioned earlier in the Order with regard to the installation of a Dean into that office. Yet the 1559 *Würtemberg Summarischer Begriff*, which adopted most of the 1547 rite's prayers, broadened the application of the rite to include it use for installing/ordaining 'Pastors, Preachers, Deacons, and Subdeacons.'"[25]

2.5 The 1569 Wolfenbüttel Church Order.

One more church order merits consideration in this context: Wolfenbüttel's Church Order of 1569. Wolfenbüttel history is noteworthy because it was not until Martin Chemnitz and Jacob Andreae conducted a visitation there in 1568 that the Reformation came to Wolfenbüttel. One result of the visitation was the production of a church order the following year.[26] Naturally, one part of the church order consisted of rites for ordination and installation. It is quite telling that Chemnitz and Andreae chose the Würtemberg Church Order as the model in this respect: "Immediately following the ordination rite the Church Order included a rite for installation entitled '*Auf welche weiss ein neuer kirchendiener von den superintenden seiner kirchen commendirt, eingeleibt and installirt werden soll.*' The rite was to be used for installing either a pastor or a deacon. The content was that of the 1547/1559 Würtemberg

---

25   ibid., p. 167.
26   ibid., p. 182–3.

Order's rite for installations, with some additions."[27] That two of the men who would later become authors of the Formula of Concord chose an installation rite which considered pastors and ordained deacons to both be serving in the same office when they might easily have revised the rite, or written their own, says much concerning their understanding of the diaconate as a grade of ministry.

In summary, although deacons are hardly even referred to in the Book of Concord, church orders used within the early Lutheran Church often made provision for the ordination of deacons, regularly considering the diaconate to be a grade of the ministry. Even Olson, an outspoken advocate of deacons of charity, concedes that "*deacon* came to designate an assistant minister in the Germanies."[28] Indeed, Olson observes that the deacon of charity was more consistently the Reformed understanding of the diaconate: "the new Protestants had reinstituted deacons who were involved in social welfare and the care of the poor. This was the ideal deacon within the Reformed tradition and in some regions where Lutheranism prevailed."[29] Smith, too, wrestles with this tension between different types of deacons: "The use of similar rites to ordain people as deacons, presbyters, elders and superintendents, particularly in Hesse, also reveals the tension experienced by Reformation churches in whether and how to articulate a distinction among different 'orders' in the church's ministry. The issue has never been resolved by churches of the Reformation traditions."[30] Again, "It is particularly clear in the work of Bugenhagen and Luther that there was to be almost no liturgically expressed distinction among deacon, presbyter or bishop."[31] Although the Braunschweig Church Order might cause one to question Smith's assessment of Bugenhagen, one

27   ibid., p. 183.
28   Olson, p. 107.
29   ibid., p. 134.
30   Smith, p. 186.
31   ibid., p. 131.

can confidently state that the Lutherans certainly did not exclude the possibility of classing the diaconate as a grade of ministry, whose members entered the ministry of Word and Sacrament like all other pastors: through call and ordination. Such an understanding of the diaconate long survived within orthodox Lutheran circles, for one finds deacons still preaching the Word and celebrating the Sacrament in Leipzig at the end of the seventeenth century:

> This chasuble was worn only by the liturgist functioning at the altar, while the other clergy wore the white surplice over the black cassock. In connection with the dedication of New Church in 1699 we are told explicitly that before the end of the musical rendering of the Kyrie, "both clergymen, namely, the head deacon in the chasuble, but Magister Werner in the surplice, came out of the sacristy." ...
>
> Each church had five clergymen, namely, "four priests, to wit, one pastor, one archdeacon, two deacons, plus a Saturday preacher, who faithfully and tirelessly performed the work of the Lord in teaching, preaching and administration of the holy sacraments according to Christ's command and institution." ...
>
> The three clergymen who functioned alongside the two chief clergymen at each main church had to preach only one sermon a week. The archdeacon, next in rank to the pastor, preached his weekly sermon at St. Nicholas on Mondays and at St. Thomas on Tuesdays, always in the customary early service. For that reason these two clergymen of the main churches were listed in the directories of Leipzig also as "archdeacon and Monday preacher" (at St. Nicholas) and "archdeacon and Tuesday preacher" (at St. Thomas)...
>
> The distribution of sermons among the pastors of the two main churches remained unchanged for generations.[32]

Thus, roughly two centuries after the beginning of the Reformation, one still finds ordained deacons celebrating the <u>sacrament and</u> preaching the Gospel within the churches of

---

32   Günther Stiller, *Johann Sebastian Bach and Liturgical Life in Leipzig,* trans. by Herbert J. A. Bouman, Daniel F. Poellot, Hilton C. Oswald, ed. by Robin A. Leaver (St. Louis: Concordia Publishing House, 1984) p. 65, 66, 67, 68.

Leipzig, one of the last orthodox cities remaining in the wake of Pietism.

3. The Ordained Diaconate in Martin Chemnitz' *Examen*.

The Jesuit assessment of Martin Chemnitz (1522-1586)—"Martin [Luther] would not have stood, if Martin [Chemnitz] had not come"—is readily accepted by many Lutheran theologians. Chemnitz' authorship of the Formula of Concord, his superintendency in the Church, and his extensive corpus of influential theological writings easily places him within the inner circle of most important theologians of the Lutheran Church. Among his writings, Chemnitz' *Examen concilii Tridentini* is particularly monumental, because it stands as a powerful Lutheran response to the Council of Trent, as well as a clear articulation of Lutheran teaching. The section "Concerning Holy Orders"[33] is especially helpful for consideration of the ordained diaconate, because Chemnitz offers an extended defense of the Lutheran understanding of grades within the ministry.

Settings forth his understanding of the duties of the office of the ministry, Chemnitz declares:

> This ministry does indeed have power, divinely bestowed (2 Cor. 10:4–6; 13:2–4), but circumscribed with certain duties and limitations, namely, to preach to Word of God, teach the erring, reprove those who sin, admonish the dilatory, comfort the troubled, strengthen the weak, resist those who speak against the truth, reproach and condemn false teaching, censure evil customs, dispense the divinely instituted sacraments, remit and retain sins, be an example to the flock, pray for the church privately and lead the church in public prayers, *be in charge of care for the poor*, publicly excommunicate the stubborn and again receive

---

33   Martin Chemnitz, *Examination of the Council of Trent*, trans. by Fred Kramer, 4 vols., vol. 2, (St. Louis: Concordia Publishing House, 1978) p. 675–714.

those who repent and reconcile them with the church, appoint pastors to the church according to the instruction of Paul, with consent of the church institute rites that serve the ministry and do not militate against the Word of God nor burden consciences but serve good order, dignity, decorum, tranquillity, edification, etc. For these are the things which belong to these two chief points, namely, to the power of order and the power of jurisdiction.[34] (Emph. added)

The list of duties set forth by Chemnitz is in many respects unremarkable; much of the list is a reiteration of the duties set forth in *Augustana* XXVIII:21. The one striking exception is the inclusion of the pastoral responsibility to "be in charge of care for the poor." The Lutheran symbols rarely include oversight of charity in lists of pastoral responsibilities, but reference is made in Treatise §80-82 to the obligation bishops have for seeing to the distribution of alms. Thus, as we shall see, Chemnitz could acknowledge care for the poor to be the deacons' primary responsibility, and still see no contradiction in recognizing the diaconate as a grade of ministry alongside the presbyterate and the episcopate.

Chemnitz also saw no contradiction between, on the one hand, the reality that an ordination into the office of the ministry included all of the duties of the office, and, on the other hand, the delegation of particular aspects of that work to various grades of the office, by human authority.[35]

The fact of the matter is this: Because many duties belong to the ministry of the church which cannot be performed by one person or by a few, when the believers are very numerous—in order, therefore, that all things may be done in an orderly way, decently, and for edification, these duties of the ministry began, as the assembly of the church grew great, to be distributed among certain ranks of ministers which they afterward called *taxeis* (ranks) or *tagmata* (orders), so

34   ibid., p. 679.
35   For the view that the "functions" should not be divided, see "A Response to an 'Overture to Establish an Ordained Diaconate,'" p. 213.

that each might have, as it were, a certain designated station in which he might serve the church in certain duties of the ministry. Thus in the beginning the apostles took care of the ministry of the Word and the sacraments and at the same time also the distribution and dispensation of alms. Afterward, however, as the number of disciples increased, they entrusted *that part of the ministry* which has also to do with alms to others, whom they called deacons. They also state the reason why they do this—that they might be able to devote themselves more diligently to the ministry of the Word and to prayer, without diversions. (Acts 6:1–4)[36] (Emph. added)

Chemnitz, as a superintendent of the Church, knew that it was not possible for every pastor in every situation to fulfill all aspects of the work of the ministry. As the Book of Concord observed that grades arose through human authority, so Chemnitz presents the rise of "ranks" or "orders" as a natural response to the growth of the Church. First, therefore, among the grades established within the office was the diaconate, to whom was committed the distribution of alms, which Chemnitz had already identified as a aspect of the work of the holy ministry. As Chemnitz observes concerning the creation of the diaconate: "This first origin of ranks or orders of ministry in the apostolic church shows what ought to be the cause, what the reason, purpose and use of such ranks or orders—that for the welfare of the assembly of the church the individual duties which belong to the ministry might be attended to more conveniently, rightly, diligently, and orderly, with a measure of dignity and for edification."[37] Thus, a church which does not allow for the establishment of "ranks or orders," when the situation of the church truly needs such grades for its own welfare, would be well served by following the apostolic example.

---

36   Chemnitz, p. 682–683.
37   ibid., p. 683.

In addition to the practical assistance the division of grades gave to the ministry by relieving the apostles of a time consuming aspect of their work, the lesser grades also provided other benefits to the Church. The establishment of grades within the office allowed ministers to be tested before being elevated to greater responsibility within the Church.

> And because the apostles afterward accepted into the ministry of teaching those from among the deacons who were approved, as Stephen and Philip, we gather that this also is a use of these ranks or orders, that men are first prepared or tested in minor duties so that afterward heavier duties may more safely and profitably be entrusted to them. That is what Paul says in 1 Tim. 3:10: "Let them also be tested first, and so let them minister." Likewise: "Those who serve well as deacons will gain a good rank for themselves."[38]

Despite the benefits of such grades within the ministry, Chemnitz reminded his readers that such grades were established by man, not God: the various ranks of bishop, presbyter, and deacon were not divinely mandated. Rather, the apostles established ranks according to Christian liberty; a liberty which carried over into the early church.[39] Furthermore, Chemnitz was adamant that his readers understand that the duties of those who occupied the various grades of ministry "were not something beside and beyond the ministry of the Word and sacraments"; to put it in modern terms, they did not occupy "auxiliary offices."

> However, because of the present dispute, the following reminder must be added: (1) that there is no command in the Word of God, which or how many such ranks or orders there should be; (2) that there were not at the time of the apostles in all churches and at all times the same number of ranks or orders, as can be

---

38   ibid..
39   "This example of the apostles the primitive church imitate reason and in similar liberty. For the grades of the duties of the ministry were disturbed, not however in identically the same way as in the church at Corinth or in that at Ephesus, but according to the circumstances obtaining in each church." (p. 685)

clearly ascertained from the epistles of Paul, written to various churches; (3) that there was not, at the time of the apostles, such a division of these ranks, but repeatedly one and the same person held and performed all the duties which belong to the ministry, as is clear from apostolic history. ... These ranks, about which we have spoken until now, were not something beside and beyond the ministry of the Word and sacraments, but the real and true duties of the ministry were distributed among certain ranks for the reasons already set forth.[40]

By making it clear that all of the ranks he had discussed thus far are part of the ministry of Word and Sacrament, Chemnitz leaves no doubt that he considered the diaconate to be one grade among many in the ministry. Furthermore, just as their work is the work of the ministry, their call to be a deacon is the same mediate, divine call as that extended to all other New Testament ministers through the voice of the Church. (The apostles, called to the ministry immediately by Christ, are the obvious exceptions.) Contrasting between the immediate and the mediate call, Chemnitz writes:

But God called few men in this immediate manner. For those who at the time of the apostles were prophets, evangelists, pastors, teachers, bishops, presbyters, and deacons were called to the ministry not immediately but by the voice of the church. Now are the things which Scripture teaches about the presence and efficacy of God through the ministry doubtful, uncertain, or false in the case of a mediate call? Surely, this is a very great and comforting promise, that Scripture declares that also that call which is issued by the voice of the church is divine, or from God. Eph. 4:11...[41]

The ranking of deacons beside bishops and pastors again underscores Chemnitz' assessment that the diaconate is, rightly understood, a lower grade of the same office. The deacons' ministry has the promise of the "presence and efficacy of God" just as surely as the promise is given to bishops and pas-

---

40   ibid.
41   ibid.., p. 706.

tors. Finally, Chemnitz argues for the fitness of the laying on of hands in ordination from the ordination of the seven in Acts 6:

> The rite of laying on hands was extraordinarily suited in this process: ...
>
> 4. That it might be signified by this visible rite that God approves the calling which is done by the voice of the church, for just as God chooses ministers by the voice of the church, so He approves the calling by the attestation of the church. Thus the calling of the deacons was approved (Acts 6:6). And thus it comes about that God bestows grace through the laying on of hands.[42]

From these words, it seems virtually indisputable that Chemnitz considered the deacons to have a divine call to the holy ministry; otherwise, their example would not support his argument. Simply put, the ordination of the deacons is proof that "God bestows grace through the laying on of hands." In this context, Chemnitz reasserts the Apology's classification of ordination as a "sacrament": "If ordination is understood in this way, of the ministry of the Word and the sacraments, as already the Apology of the Augsburg Confession explained the position of our churches, then we have no objection to calling ordination a sacrament. And there the words are added, 'We shall not object either to calling the laying on of hands a sacrament.'"[43] Clearly, ordination is not an 'empty rite' for Chemnitz, and yet he also sets forth the ordination of the deacons as a prime example of ordination into the holy ministry.

In conclusion, therefore, it becomes clear that Chemnitz readily accepts that the diaconate is a grade within the office of holy ministry, not a separate, 'sub-clerical' office. Although he accepts the position that the work of deacons is primarily connected with charity, Chemnitz classifies such work as an aspect of the ministry. Since the ordination of the deacons is proof that God bestows blessings upon pastors through

---

42   ibid., p. 693.
43   ibid., p. 694.

ordination, Chemnitz clearly supported the practice of continuing to ordain them, especially in light of his role in formulating the Wolfenbüttel Church Order (see section 3.5).

4. The Ordained Diaconate in the *Loci Theologici* of Johann Gerhard.˘

Recognized as "the 'arch-theologian' and standard dogmatician of the Lutheran Church,"[44] Johann Gerhard (1582–1637) is best known for his expansive dogmatics textbook, the *Loci Theologici*. Written over a twelve year period (1609–1621), the *Loci* influenced generations of Lutheran theologians and pastors. The nine volumes of the *Loci* provide a thorough examination of virtually any imaginable theological issue or topic up through Gerhard's time, and so the chapter on the ministry (Locus XXIII) is one of the most lengthy in the entire dogmatics. For purposes of this study, analysis of Gerhard's understanding of the diaconate and grades of ministry will be limited to this locus.[45]

Gerhard, like Chemnitz before him, firmly upheld the Lutheran understanding that there were grades within the ministry—grades which were established by human authority. Thus, Gerhard took offense at Bellarmine's charge that the Lutherans had fallen into the heresy of Aerius by making no distinction between bishops and elders. Gerhard responded: "First, that Aerius, as Epiphanius witnesses, was 'a complete Arian.' Second, none of us says: 'There is no difference between a bishop and an elder.' Instead, we acknowledge that in order to encourage good order and harmony in the church, it is useful to preserve the distinction between bishops and el-

44   "Gerhard, Johann," Lutheran Cyclopedia, p. 196.
45   We are indebted to Dr. Richard Dinda for his unpublished translation of Gerhard's *Loci* (a copy of which is available on microfiche in the library of Concordia Theological Seminary in Fort Wayne, Indiana). All references to Gerhard's locus will be by paragraph number, since Dr. Dinda kept his enumeration consistent with those found in the Edward Preus edition of 1885.

ders.'" (§243) The forcefulness of Gerhard's statement brings to mind Philip Melanchthon's words from the Apology of the Augsburg Confession that it was "our greatest wish to maintain church polity": Gerhard wanted it to be clearly understood that his generation had not changed its assessment concerning the canonical polity, citing Gregory of Valencia as proof that the Lutherans still had bishops; they simply called them "superintendents." (§243) Earlier in Locus XXIII, Gerhard explained the Lutheran concept of grades as follows:

> Although we vehemently disapprove of the lawlessness and destructiveness of those who remove ranking from the ministry of the church because it is a source of discord and of every evil; in our churches we retain and decree that we must retain ranking among ministers, so that some are bishops, some elders and some deacons, etc. First, with the variety and difference of gifts God Himself creates a ranking among ministers. We notice this diversity of gifts not only in ministers of the primitive church but also in those of the church today. ... Third, in the church we should do all things "decently and in order," 1 Cor. 14:40. That orderliness, however, requires ranking among ministers of the church lest confusions arise. In that correct controlling of every assembly there is required the ranking of those who are in charge. The same thing, therefore, is required in the assembly of the church. Fourth, the establishment of a ranking among ministers of the church contributes to harmony and unity, keeps us from fearing the disorders arising from the egotism and ambition of inferior ministers and places a restraint on the rashness of those who try to disturb the peace of the church. Fifth, on the basis of ranking and grades of ministers, this convenience also occurs, that these can first be tested in the case of lower ministers who are going to be promoted to higher grades. 1 Tim. 3:13: "Those who serve well as deacons gain a good standing for themselves." (§205)

Thus we see that Gerhard appeals to the same points which were emphasized by Chemnitz: grades of ministry offer an opportunity for those in the lower grades to be tested before they are advanced in the Church; grades are necessary to maintaining order within the Church. However, Gerhard's assessment that grades are divinely created "with the variety and difference of gifts" needs to be rightly understood. Gerhard is not saying that the grades are different offices, but rather that the requirements of the different grades reflect the varying abilities which God has given to those who hold the office. Indeed, the diaconate is specifically referenced as a lower grade of ministry which is preparatory for the higher grades. Gerhard's understanding that some grades of ministry are higher than others does mean that some have greater or more duties than others by divine right. Rather, Gerhard upholds the understanding that all who serve in the ministry have, by divine right, all of the same duties, even if, according to human right, they belong to a lower grade of office and thus perform more or fewer duties, according to their grade:

> First, we must distinguish the power of the ministry and of its jurisdiction from the order or, as some say, from the power of the order. After all, although there are diverse orders in the ministry of the church, the power of the ministry in the preaching of the Word and the administration of the sacraments and the power of jurisdiction which consists of the use of the keys belongs to all ministers equally. Consequently, the Word is preached, the sacraments are administered and absolution is pronounced by a man who has been legitimately called to the ministry of the church, even though he belongs to the lowest rank of the ministry. Those are as valid and effective as if the greatest bishop, prophet or apostle preached the Word, administered those sacraments and pronounced that absolution. ... Second, that diversity of grades certainly does depend on divine right by reason of its genus, that to the extent that it is necessary for good order and tranquillity in the church there are some distinct grades; then, by reason of gifts to the extent that by the very variety and diversity of gifts God declares that He wants distinct grades to be arranged among ministers; then, by reason of some grades in particular, to the extent that He distinguishes the office of prophets and apostles from the

other grades and prefers them thereto. On the other hand, however, one cannot say absolutely and generally in regard to all the grades of ministers of the church that their institution and distinction depend on divine institution. (§206)

Thus, although God gives varying abilities to different pastors, and while they may therefore be better fitted on an individual basis for varying grades of ministry, Gerhard's point is that God does not establish the particular grades (e.g., bishop, presbyter, and deacon) by name. Regardless of how many ranks are established and what they are called, the ministry is one office, with the same divinely-given, "valid and effective" Word and Sacrament. Although Roman Catholic opponents such as Bellarmine might insist that variety of duties and offices are divinely established, Gerhard insists that "The distinction between elders and deacons, however, was unknown to the apostles. In fact, Paul calls all ministers of the church, whether bishops, elders or deacons, 'stewards of the mysteries of God,' 1 Cor. 4:1." (§16) Here Gerhard eliminates any doubt regarding his understanding of the diaconate: it is fully a part of the ministry of Word and Sacrament and deacons are as fully "stewards of the mysteries of God" as the bishops and presbyters because of their call and ordination to the ministry.

Although the Lutherans do use the term "ecclesiastical order," Gerhard wants it understood that such order, although God-pleasing, did not mean that any grade of ministry failed to fully participate in the one office. "...[T]he title 'ecclesiastical order' reminds us of the distinct levels of persons whom God has placed in charge of the church's ministry. You see, although all ministers have the same condition as far as spiritual power and jurisdiction are concerned, divine providence nevertheless wanted distinct levels and orders to exist among them, as we shall show later in greater detail." (§5) Gerhard's concern is the same as that of the Reformers: defending the legitimacy of the ministry of Lutheran pastors, despite the fact that Roman Catholic bishops did not ordain them. The division of grades of ministry is to serve the Church, not to be lorded over lower grades of ministry. Thus, the title of "minister" may be used in several ways to refer to those who hold the office:

> The title "ministers" which we said earlier is concrete, occurs variously and in different ways. We can divide into the following classes: first, some are established as general, competent for every ministry of the church, but some are special, suited only for a particular order or rank of ministers. Here we must learn that in many titles that two-fold meeting concurs so that sometimes they are taken in the general sense and sometimes in the special sense. This is very obvious from the names "prophets," "bishops," "deacons," etc. (§13)

In discussing the topic of the mediate call, Gerhard argues (as Chemnitz had before him) for the divine origin of the call from the example of the call and ordination of the deacons of Acts 6. Gerhard notes "Regarding the mediate call we must treat two points in particular: first that it is no less divine than the immediate call; second, what those ordinary means are which God wants to use for the mediate call." (§83) Gerhard's examination of Acts 6:3 follows his treatment of Acts 1:23 as an example of apostolic practice concerning a mediate call:

> In Acts 6:3, when they had to select deacons, Peter says to the entire crowd of disciples: "Therefore, brethren, pick out from among you seven men of good repute, full of the Spirit and of wisdom, whom we may appoint to this duty. V. 5–6: "And what they said pleased the whole multitude, and they chose Stephen ... and Philip, etc. These they set before the apostles, and they prayed and laid their hands on them. Observe here, first, that Peter and the apostles defer the business of appointing deacons to the entire church; second, the church approves this plan of the apostles; third, the selection of deacons was not made by the apostles alone but by the entire church; fourth, not only the apostles but also the old men placed their hands on them in the name of

the rest of the church. Regarding the last we draw a probable conclusion from 1 Tim. 4:14: "Do not neglect the gift which you have which was given to you ... when the elders laid their hands on you." Here we take the word "elders" to mean not only those who labor in the Word but also the old men acting on behalf of the rest of the church. It is quite likely, therefore, that the same practice was observed in the selection of the deacons. Even if we were to concede, however, that only the apostles laid their hands on the deacons, nothing from our argument would fail because through this laying on of hands they also at the same time bore witness that they considered the selection of the deacons as ratified by the suffrage of the church. (§92)

Gerhard's arguments about the "old men" of the Church aside, the germane point for our study is that Gerhard saw no difference between the ordination bestowed on the deacons in Acts 6 and the gift-bestowing ordination of which St. Paul reminds St. Timothy in 1 Tim. 4:14. Again, clearly Gerhard is operating from the understanding that the diaconate is a grade of the one office of the holy ministry.

Gerhard's examination of the term "deacon" offered him an opportunity to explore the manner in which this particular grade of ministry came into existence and spread throughout the Church:

Third, in a more special sense, it [the term "deacon"] is taken for those who had been occupied chiefly with that part of the ministry of the church which was involved with the food and distribution of necessities. As a result they are called "ministers of the tables"; that is, those who distribute to each person the necessities of life from the communal goods. Acts 6:1–4 ... On the basis of this passage appears the occasion for introducing the order of deacons into the church. But because that gathering of goods occurred only in the church at Jerusalem, however, but was never brought into the churches of the gentiles who had been converted to Christ, it consequently happened that those were called deacons who had the care of the poor, the sick and the pilgrims in the church, not from goods gathered in common but from those collected in the churches. ... Finally, those deacons were commissioned with the ordinary responsibilities of teaching (from which also those whom Acts 6 mentions were not simply excluded, although they were chiefly in charge of tables), so that they were allied with the elders in preaching the Word, administering the sacraments, visiting the sick, etc. Thus, for this reason they became teachers of a lower order in the church. Likewise, in Phil. 1:1 deacons are connected with bishops or elders; and, after the apostle described the virtues of a bishop, he added the things that are required in deacons, that is, in ministers of a lower order. 1 Tim. 3:8: "Deacons likewise must be serious, etc." In v. 13 he adds: "Those who serve well as deacons," who perform their function uprightly and faithfully in that lower grade of ministry, "gain a good standing for themselves"; that is, they will be able to be elevated to greater things later. (§30)

Again, it must be noted that Gerhard considered overseeing charity as a "part of the ministry..." Also, he is insistent that the deacons of Acts 6 "were not simply excluded" from the teaching ministry, but rather "they were allied with the elders in preaching the Word, administering the sacraments, visiting the sick, etc." Thus Philip and Stephen were ordained into the one office, began with exercising one aspect of the work of the ministry—administering charity—and later were trusted with more elements of the work of the ministry:

> ... the apostles selected Philip along with six others as deacons and laid their hands on them, Acts 6:5–6. Although it is the special duty of deacons "to serve the tables," v. 2, that is, to provide the faithful with the necessary sustenance in that communion of good people, we conclude, nevertheless, that the office of teaching was not removed and kept apart from them from that which is noted about Stephen, who belonged to the same order of deacons, v. 8–9: "Stephen, full of grace and power, did great wonders and signs among the people," and he debated with the opponents of truth who "could not withstand the wisdom and

the Spirit with which he spoke." If the office of teaching along with serving the tables had not been committed at the same time to the deacons, why would there have been a need to investigate in the election of deacons men "filled with the Holy Spirit and with wisdom," v. 3? Surely such great gifts of the Holy Spirit and such wisdom, that is, so substantial a knowledge of heavenly doctrine, would not have been required for a simple ministry to tables. (§68)

Thus Gerhard considers the status of the Acts 6 deacons to be essentially self-evident; the candidates were examined for their knowledge of "heavenly doctrine"—a knowledge which is not necessary to work in a soup kitchen or for 'meals on wheels' (which is not to diminish the importance of overseeing such charitable work). Rather, the seven were specifically chosen, Gerhard says, because their knowledge of the Scriptures made it possible that they were "apt to teach": "It is false, however, that deacons are merely in charge of tables, for we have shown earlier from the example of Stephen and Philip that they, too, performed the duty of teaching." (§92)

Gerhard ultimately concludes that one may speak of "two kinds of deacons"—one centered in works of charity, the other fully devoted to the work of teaching and administering the Sacraments:

Likewise, there are two kinds of deacons, so-called from their ministering. Some discharged the concern for the poor and the distribution thereto of the goods of the church. Acts 6:2 describes their origin. In 1 Cor. 12:28 they are called "helps" or "helpers," because they would provide help from the alms and collections for the poor, widows, orphans and pilgrims. They were like stewards of the church, then, to whom today correspond the prefects of the church treasury. On the other hand, some were joined to the bishops or elders in the function of teaching and of administering the sacraments in order to supplement their duties and alleviate their difficulties. In this way they are connected to bishops in Phil. 1:1 and 1 Tim. 3:8. There are those who think that the

128

office of deacons is clearly separate from the responsibility of teaching because the disciples deny that they can be free to serve tables and to minister the Word simultaneously, Acts 6:2, and because Paul requires in a bishop that he be "apt to teach," but in a deacon only that he "must hold the mystery of faith with a clear conscience," 1 Tim. 3:2 and 9. We must distinguish, however, between times and parts of a duty. Certainly, in the church at Jerusalem deacons were first established for this purpose, that they have the care of tables, that is, that in the sharing of the goods they serve an equal distribution of foods. Later, however, with the passage of time they were also placed in charge in other churches of conducting assemblies for the people, as Jerome witnesses in a letter to the deacon Rusticus. Consequently, the apostle requires in a deacon almost the same talent as he requires in a bishop. ... Because the deacons were distributing to the poor from those collections, it next happened, therefore, that they were also moved up to the administration of the Eucharist (which they celebrated with the same collections) and finally even to the preaching of the Word, as is agreed from Justin, *apol. 2, pro Christ.* Too, this is not to mention the fact that not even those first deacons of the church at Jerusalem were completely and absolutely excluded from the office of teaching, as we have shown earlier §68 with the examples of Stephen and Philip. (§233)

Thus Gerhard contends that the earliest apostolic institution of deacons (Acts 6) was dedicated to that aspect of the ministry involved in works of charity; later references to deacons— specifically Phil. 1 and 1 Tim. 3—speak of those deacons fully involved in Word and Sacrament. This development occurred, Gerhard reasons, as deacons went from works of charity, to celebrating the Lord's Supper to "finally even" preaching. Still, even at this point Gerhard does not concede that the Acts 6 deacons were not in the the office of the holy ministry, for "not even those first deacons of the church at Jerusalem were completely and absolutely excluded..."

In conclusion, therefore, one finds that Gerhard's comments regarding the status of deacons within the Church are even more direct than Chemnitz'. Gerhard's declaration that "The distinction between elders and deacons, however, was unknown to the apostles. In fact, Paul calls all ministers of the church, whether bishops, elders or deacons, 'stewards of the mysteries of God,' 1 Cor. 4:1" (§16)—is completely uncompromising in its view that the diaconate is a grade of the ministry. Just as vigorously as Gerhard defends the existence of grades within the ministry, so firmly does he maintain that such grades are by human rite. The bishop does not, by divine right, have more duties than a deacon; instead, the deacon simply exercises fewer aspects of the work of the ministry until he "gained a good standing" for himself.

5. The Ordained Diaconate in the *Theologia didactico-polemica* of Johann Andreas Quenstedt.

Johann Andreas Quenstedt (1617–1688) and his Theologia didactico-polemica are worthy of consideration in this study for several reasons. First, it has been observed that "Johann Quenstedt ranks after Martin Chemnitz (1522–1586) and Johann Gerhard (1582–1637) as probably the most influential Lutheran leader in the post-Reformation era."[46] Second, the publication of his *Theologia* 155 years after the Diet of Augsburg readily demonstrates that it is the product of an unquestionably "mature" Lutheran theology.

Consistent with his methodology throughout the *Theologia,* Quenstedt divides the chapter on the ministry into two portions: didactic and polemic. The didactic portion of the chapter consists of a series of theses, briefly expounded by notes. The fourteenth, and final, thesis of the didactic portion

---

46   Johann Andreas Quenstedt, *The Nature and Character of Theology,* ed. and trans. by Luther Poellot, (St. Louis: Concordia Publishing House, 1986) p. 9.

of the chapter on the ministry states: "Adjuncts are necessity, dignity, usefulness, call, ordination, grades of ministers, etc."[47] Thus the final section of this last thesis declares:

> (VI) Grades of ministers. We retain order among ministers in our church, so that some are bishops, others presbyters, [and] others deacons, because both in the apostolic and in the primitive church there were distinct orders of ministers, and they divinely established, 1 Co. 12:28; Eph. 4:11. Yet we say that the same power of the ministry in the preaching of the Word and in the administration of the sacraments and the power of jurisdiction consisting in the use of the keys belongs to all ministers of the church.[48]

Quenstedt's explanation of grades of ministers makes it clear that his understanding is consistent with that of both Chemnitz and Gerhard: bishops, presbyters and deacons are all grades of ministry which, despite differences in responsibilities in according to human rite, share the "same power of ministry" consisting of Word, Sacrament, and the keys ("power of jurisdiction"). The same thesis states that "Ordination, by which in the sight of God and in the presence of the whole church, through the laying on of hands the person legitimately called is commended to God with prayers [and] inaugurated into the holy office and public testimony is borne to the preceding call."[49]

The matter of ordination, and who may validly ordain candidates for the ministry, was still an important theological question in Quenstedt's time. In the "Polemic" section of Quenstedt's chapter on the ministry, question IV takes up the topic, "Is There True Ecclesiastical Order in Lutheran Churches?" Quenstedt defends the thesis, "In the churches of the Lutherans there is true ecclesiastical order and a legitimate call of ministers, and thus there are also true pastors there," observing:

47   Johann Andreas Quenstedt, *The Holy Ministry*, ed. and trans. by Luther Poellot, (Fort Wayne: Concordia Theological Seminary Press, 1991) p. 6.
48   ibid.
49   ibid.

The papists, who oppose us in this, falsely suppose (1) that bishops are by divine right superior to presbyters both with regard to order and with regard to jurisdiction, or that the episcopate and the presbytery are distinct orders by divine right in such a way that only a bishop can perform very many functions that a presbyter is not allowed to perform. (2) The function of ordaining belongs only to a bishop by divine right. But both are false. For (1) the distinction between bishops and presbyters, of which the papists dream and the Romanizing Britains pretend, is not of divine precept but only of human institution, that is, it is absolutely not by special institution of Christ and the apostles or founded in Scripture, but introduced by human counsel, as we will prove elsewhere. (2) It is also false that ordination is divinely committed only to bishops or that the function of ordaining belongs only to bishops by divine right, but that ordination performed by a presbyter is void and invalid by divine right. For by divine right no difference was made between a bishop and a presbyter with regard to authority to ordain, but this function of ordaining belongs to both by divine right. ... The primitive church also in all places regarded as valid the ordinations not only of deacons or presbyters but also bishops performed by presbyters, as David Blondel points out, through eight preceding centuries.[50]

Thus it can be clearly seen that Quenstedt, like Chemnitz and Gerhard before him, continued to uphold the ordination of deacons, and defended the equality of grades of the office. Still, over 150 years after the Diet of Augsburg, Quenstedt maintained that the Lutherans did not lightly depart from submitting to canonical authority; rather, "For since the papistic bishops did not want to ordain the ministers of our churches unless they returned to the bosom of Roman Thais, it was better to ordain without bishops than that the church completely lack presbyters. For where bishops degenerate into wolves, there presbyters reclaim their ancient right to ordain

---

50   ibid., p. 31.

and consecrate with good reason."[51] Although the grades are of human origin, still, Gerhard observed, Lutherans are not followers of Aerius.

Conclusion.

Undeniably, the history of the diaconate is complicated. Some have applied the title to a lay office devoted to works of charity, others have seen the office as a 'sub-clerical' one. For several of the most significant 16th and 17th century Lutheran theologians, however, the diaconate was understood to be something else: a grade of the one office of the holy ministry, the ministry of Word and Sacrament.

Although it is true that the Lutheran confessions never explicitly declare the diaconate to be one of the grades of ministry, Reformation-era Lutheran church orders offer examples of ordained deacons functioning in Word and Sacrament ministry. Martin Chemnitz, one of the authors of the Formula of Concord, understood the deacons to be ordained into that ministry and that "God bestows grace through the laying on of hands."[52] The most important Lutheran theologians of the 17th century, Johann Gerhard and Johann Quenstedt, also defended the ordination of deacons, as well as the understanding that the diaconate is one grade of the ministry, which shares in all the blessings and responsibilities of that office.

In light of all of the evidence examined, it is clearly established that an ordained diaconate serving in Word and Sacrament ministry is consistent with theology of the orthodox Lutheran fathers and was reflected in the Church's practice in the 16th and 17th centuries. This does not mean, however, that every proposal for an ordained diaconate should automatically be seen as prudent or consistent with orthodox

---

51   ibid., p. 32.
52   Chemnitz, p. 693.

Lutheran doctrine and practice. The orthodox fathers understood that any limitation on the work of a grade of ministry was by human, not divine right: ordination to any grade of ministry was ordination into the whole ministry. Furthermore, just because such a grade may be established, does not mean that it is necessarily wise to do so in every circumstance. The grades of ministry should aid "good order" in the Church and should serve the edification of the Body of Christ.

Pastoral Responsibility and the Office of the Keys in the Book of Concord

That the prime Act of Power enstated by *Christ* on his *Apostles*, as for the *governing* of the *Church*, (and exorcising or banishing all devils out of it) so for the effectual performing that great act of Charity to mens souls, reducing pertinacious sinners to repentance, should be so either wholly dilapidated, or piteously deformed, as to continue in the *Church* only under one of these two notions, either of an empty piece of *formality*, or of an *engine of State*, and saecular contrivance, (the true *Christian* use of *shaming* sinners into reformation, being well-nigh vanished out of *Christendome*) might by an alien, or an heathen, much more by the pondering *Christian*, be conceived very strange and unreasonable, were it not a title clear, that we are faln into those times of which it was foretold by two *Apostles*, that in *these last dayes, there should come scoffers, walking after their own lusts*: the *Pride* and contumacy (which have almost become the *Genius*) of this profane polluted age, heightning men to an *Atheistical* fearlesse *scoffing* and scorning of all that pretends to work any cures, to lay any restraint on them, to rob them of any degree of that licentiousnesse, which is become the very religion, and doctrine of some (under the disguise of *Christian liberty*) and (*the Lord be merciful unto us*) the practise of most rankes of *Christian Professors*.[1]

Almost all observers (regardless of their personal theological convictions) understand that the Lutheran Church—Missouri Synod (LC—MS) is in a state of crisis. There is a great deal of debate on various matters related to this situation, such as the *origin* and *duration* of the crisis; whether it's nature is *political*, *theological*, or both; whether it may be

1   [Harry Hammond,] *Of the Power of the Keyes: or, Of Binding and Loosing,* London, Printed for Richard Royston, at the Angel in Ivie-Lane. 1647, A 1

resolved within the current synodical structure or whether it must necessarily lead to a split. Nevertheless, despite such debates, the fact of the crisis remains.

In this paper, the presenter will endeavor to set forth what he believes to be one of the primary sources of the crisis, and the responsibility which rests upon pastors to confront the doctrinal error which has given rise to so many years of conflict. It is our contention that the Missourian crisis rests in a fundamental error concerning the nature of the pastoral office. To state the matter succinctly, the crisis in the LC—MS strikes as the very heart of the pastoral office because it is rooted in an effort to undermine—even eliminate—pastoral responsibility for the exercise of the office of the keys. The clear teaching of the Book of Concord has been set aside in a return to what are essentially self-appointed bishops in the offices of district presidents, who imagine themselves, especially in light of resolutions adopted at the 2004 convention of the synod, to have ultimate authority over the binding and loosing of sin within the Church. This unscriptural situation cannot be tolerated within Christ's Church. The Church's enduring confession in such a situation is set forth in the clear words of the Treatise on the Power and Primacy of the Pope:

> Since, therefore, bishops have tyrannically transferred this jurisdiction to themselves alone, and have basely abused it, there is no need, because of this jurisdiction, to obey bishops. But since the reasons why we do not obey are just, it is right also to restore this jurisdiction to godly pastors [to whom, by Christ's command it belongs], and to see to it that it be legitimately exercised for the reformation of life and the glory of God. (¶76)[2]

---

2   Note: all English citations from the Book of Concord are from the H. E. Jacobs edition (Decatur, Illinois: The Johann Gerhard Institute, 1996).

Pastoral Responsibility and the Reformation

Lutherans are taught from childhood to celebrate Martin Luther's *Ninety-Five Theses* as a bold confession against papal indulgences, but they rarely give much thought to the actual *reason* why such a stand was necessary for Luther. The Lutheran Reformation began because of a conflict over the connection between pastoral responsibility and the office of the keys—Luther's conflict with the papacy began because he protested papal interference in the pastor's ability to carry out his office. As H. E. Jacobs observed in his biography of Luther: "[The 95 Theses] were the outcome of his pastoral fidelity to the souls with whom he had to deal in the confessional. ... His criticism was called forth, not by papal Indulgences in themselves, but what he had found to be their abuse in a specific case falling under his pastoral jurisdiction."[3] Heiko Oberman also emphasized the pastoral nature of Luther's concerns regarding indulgences: "This whole indulgences issue, this selling of insurance as protection against the wrath of God is the appalling consequence of Rome's assiduous efforts at securing inward and outward dominion over the people of God. ... Luther's comment: 'Never before has the Church been so desolate.'"[4] Oberman noted that although indulgences left in place the *form* of the traditional rite of confession, they emptied it of its *substance*: "Plenary indulgences, which only the pope could offer, promised the complete remission of punishment and sin, so that though a visit to the confessional was still necessary, contrition, the condition for forgiveness of sin, could be proven by the possession of a plenary indulgence."[5] With contrition taken for granted if one possessed a plenary indulgence, and no need for further works of satisfaction, pas-

---

3   Henry Eyster Jacobs, *Martin Luther: The Hero of the Reformation*, (New York and London: G. P. Putnam's Son, 1902) p. 59–60.

4   Heiko A. Oberman, *Luther: Man between God and the Devil*, trans. by Eileen Walliser-Schwarzbart, (New Haven & London: Yale University Press, 1989) p. 72.

5   ibid., p. 75–77.

toral jurisdiction was emptied of any meaning or substance.[6] Luther's theses directly confronted such papal interference in pastoral jurisdiction. Thus we read, for example:

> 5. The pope has neither the will nor the power to remit any penalties beyond those imposed either at his own discretion or by canon law.
>
> 6. The pope himself cannot remit guilt, but only declare and confirm that it has been remitted by God; or, at most, he can remit it in cases reserved to his discretion. Except for these cases, the guilt remains untouched.
>
> 7. God never remits guilt to anyone without, at the same time, making him humbly submissive to the priest, His representative.[7]

The pastoral relationship expressed in thesis 7 is central to the catechism's explanation of absolution. In his Small Catechism, Dr. Luther cut through the Gordian knot of 'reserved cases,' indulgences, and the rest of papal interference with a single question and answer: "What is confession? *Answer.* Confession consists of two parts: the one is, that we confess our sins; the other, that we receive absolution or forgiveness through the pastor [*Beichtiger / confitemur*] as of God Himself, in no wise doubting, but firmly believing that our sins are thus forgiven before God in heaven." (SC Of Confession.16) Whereas the papacy presents the person of the pope as *the* vicar of Christ on Earth, Luther's catechesis instructed the Christian that Christ is active throughout the Church through the office of the ministry of Word and Sacrament. Thus the Church confesses in *Augustana* V: "That we may obtain this faith, the Office of Teaching the Gospel and administering the Sacraments was instituted. For through the Word and Sacraments as through Instruments, the Holy Ghost is given, who worketh faith where and when it pleaseth God in them

---

6   Plenary indulgences thus created a situation in the Church which is analogous to have immunity from discipline for one's sinful actions because one had permission from one's ecclesiastical supervisor.

7   in *Martin Luther: Selections from his writings*, ed. by John Dillenberger (Garden City, New York: Anchor Books, 1961) p. 490–1.

that hear the Gospel..." (¶1–2) And *Augustana* VII defines the Church as that *congregatio sanctorum* gathered around the proper exercise of that office: "The Church is the congregation of saints, in which the Gospel is rightly taught and the Sacraments rightly administered." (¶1) Or in Luther's words of the Smalcald Articles: "For, thank God, to-day a child seven years old knows what the Church is, viz. saints, believers and lambs who hear the voice of their Shepherd." (III.XII.2) The voice of the Shepherd is heard in the 'spoken Word' proclaimed by the called servants of the Lord. Thus Luther declared: "Therefore in regard to this we ought and must constantly maintain that God does not wish to deal with us otherwise than through the spoken Word and sacraments, and that whatever without the Word and sacraments is extolled as spirit is the devil himself." (SA III.X.10)

The Christian is directed to his pastor so that he may receive forgiveness: "Moreover, the power of the keys administers and presents the Gospel through absolution, which is the true voice of the Gospel. ... And because God truly quickens through the Word, the keys truly remit sins before God, according to Luke 10:16: 'He that heareth you heareth Me.' Wherefore the voice of the one absolving must be believed not otherwise than we would believe a voice from heaven." (AP XII.39, 40) And Luther teaches that the responsibility for rebuking evil resides with pastors: "Thus you see, in short, it is forbidden to speak any evil of our neighbor, and yet the civil government, preachers, father and mother are excepted, that this commandment may be so understood that evil be not unreproved. ... For here necessity requires one to speak of the evil, to make accusation, to investigate and testify;" (LC 8th Commandment.274–5).

Perhaps it is hard for modern man, living in an age of denominationalism and large institutional churches, to fully grasp the radical character of the Evangelical Lutheran understanding of the ministry and the Church. The Lutheran Confessions certainly do not deny that orthodox Christians recognize fellowship with one another, and express such fellowship in ecclesiastical structures, with, it should be remembered, a marked preference for an episcopal polity ("... we will gladly maintain ecclesiastical and canonical order, provided the bishops only cease to rage against our Churches." ([AP XIV:28]). Nevertheless, the identification of "Church" is first, and primarily, applied to the *congregatio sanctorum* gathered around the faithful exercise of the office of the ministry. In the words of the Apology: "And we know that the Church is with those who teach the Word of God aright, and administer the sacraments aright, and not with those who not only by their edicts endeavor to efface God's Word, but also put to death those who teach what is right and true;..." (XIV:27)

Throughout the Lutheran Confessions, the link between the office of the keys and pastoral responsibility is expressed primarily on the parish level. The episcopate may be established as a visible (even preferable) representation of the unity of those united in doctrine and practice. But the Lutheran Confessions clearly teach that the bishop *does not* possess any higher authority with regard to pastoral jurisdiction. Thus we confess in the Treatise on the Power and Primacy of the Pope:

> "For with the exception of ordination, what does the bishop that the elder [presbyter] does not?" Jerome therefore teaches that it is by human authority that the grades of bishop and elder or pastor are distinct. And the subject itself declares this, because the power is the same, as he has said above. But one matter afterwards made a distinction between bishops and pastors, viz. ordination, because it was so arranged that one bishop might ordain ministers in a number of churches. But since by divine authority the grades of bishop and pastor are not diverse, it is manifest that ordination by a pastor in his own church has been appointed by divine law [if a pastor in his own church ordain

certain suitable persons to the ministry, such ordination is, according to divine law, undoubtedly effective and right]. (Treatise ¶62–65)

Again, the Treatise explicitly maintains that responsibility for jurisdiction resides in the pastoral office: "The Gospel has assigned to those who preside over churches the command to teach the Gospel, to remit sins, to administer the sacraments, and besides jurisdiction, viz. the command to excommunicate those whose crimes are known, and again of absolving the repenting. And by the confession of all, even of the adversaries, it is clear that this power by divine right is common to all who preside over churches, whether they be called pastors, or elders, or bishops." (¶60–61) Thus we see that "divine law"[8] assigns ordination to "a pastor in his own church"[9]. Again, "divine right"[10] has assigned[11] jurisdiction (the binding and loosing of sins through absolution and excommunication) to the pastoral office. This passage therefore explains the intention of *Augustana* XXVIII where we confess:

> ...that the power of the Keys, or the power of the bishops, according to the Gospel, is a power or commandment of God, to preach the Gospel, to remit and retain sins, and to administer sacraments. For with that commandment, Christ sends forth His Apostles [John 20:21ssq.]: "As My Father has sent Me, even so send I you. Receive ye the Holy Ghost. Whosesoever sins ye remit, they are remitted unto them; and whosesoever sins ye retain, they are retained." (¶5–6)

The Apology declares in the same article: "But we are speaking of a bishop according to the Gospel. ... Therefore the bishop has the power of the order, i.e. the ministry of the Word and sacraments; he has also the power of jurisdiction, i.e. the authority to excommunicate those guilty of open crimes, and

---

8   *jure divino*
9   *manifestum est ordinationem a pastore in sua ecclesia factam jure divino ratam esse*
10   *jure divino*
11   *tribuit*

141

again to absolve them if they are converted and seek absolution." (¶13)

Thus we see that in *Augustana* XXVIII we use the term 'bishop' as it is used in Holy Scripture: to refer to the *one office* of the holy ministry. However, in the Treatise, the term 'bishop' is used to refer to that *grade* established by human authority[12] within the one office. The Lutheran Confessions thus do not concede any other authority to the grade of office referred to as 'bishop' than to perform ordinations as a visible expression of unity in doctrine and practice: "We have spoken of ordination, which alone, as Jerome says, distinguished bishops from other elders. Therefore there is need of no discussion concerning the other duties of bishops. Nor is it indeed necessary to speak of confirmation, nor of consecration of bells, which are almost the only other things which they have retained." (Treatise ¶73)

Throughout the confessions, the authority to loose and bind are treated always mentioned together as responsibilities of the office of the ministry. One is never left with the sense that the pastor has authority to loose the sins of the repentant, but requires 'approval' from any third party to bind the sins of the impenitent. The symbols specifically repudiate the idea that bishops have a higher authority concerning the exercise of the office of the keys.

The Roman notion that bishops have a higher authority with regard to the office of the keys is emphatically rejected in the Lutheran Confessions: "It is manifest that the common jurisdiction of excommunicating those guilty of manifest crimes belongs to all pastors. This they [i.e., the bishops] have tyrannically transferred to themselves alone, and have applied it to the acquisition of gain." (Treatise ¶74) Such tyranny in the Church is sufficient grounds to refuse obedience to such bish-

---

12   *humana autoritate*

ops, to overturn their usurpation of pastoral jurisdiction, and to restore the office of the keys to those to whom the Lord of the Church entrusted that responsibility.

> Since, therefore, bishops have tyrannically transferred this jurisdiction to themselves alone, and have basely abused it, there is no need, because of this jurisdiction, to obey bishops. But since the reasons why we do not obey are just, it is right also to restore this jurisdiction to godly pastors [to whom, by Christ's command it belongs], and to see to it that it be legitimately exercised for the reformation of life and the glory of God. (¶76)

The argument set forth with the posting of the *Ninety-Five Theses* reached its final confessional formulation in the Treatise. Interference in pastoral jurisdiction is one of the central reasons why the authority of the pope, and those bishops who submit to him, is rejected.

> Since, therefore the bishops, who are devoted to the Pope, defend godless doctrines and godless services, and do not ordain godly teachers, yea aid the cruelty of the Pope, and besides have wrested the jurisdiction from pastors, and exercise this only tyrannically [for their own profit]; and lastly, since in matrimonial cases they observe many unjust laws; the reasons why the churches do not recognize these as bishops are sufficiently numerous and necessary. (¶79)

The early Lutheran fathers clearly properly understood the nature of pastoral jurisdiction, a fact readily documented from the writings of several of the formulators of Concord. As authors of the Formula of Concord, their insights into the whole of the Lutheran Confessions are of particular value. Therefore we will take a brief look at two works by David Chytraeus and Martin Chemnitz.

David Chytraeus wrote his *Summary of the Christian Faith* in 1568 as a textbook for the catechetical instruction of young men. In that work, Chytraeus set forth absolution, excommunication, and the office of the keys as follows:

What is absolution?

Absolution is the announcement of the forgiveness of sins by which the minister of the Gospel bears witness in the name of Christ that the person who repents of his sins and asks for pardon has been released and is free from sin, the wrath of God, and eternal condemnation.

What is excommunication?

Excommunication is the official declaration of the wrath of God and of eternal damnation by which the minister of the Gospel in the name of Christ states that sinners who were admonished and are not confessing their sins nor asking for pardon are guilty of the wrath of God and of eternal damnation, excludes them from the fellowship of the Church and hands them over to Satan for the destruction of the flesh that the spirit might be saved, Matt. 18, 1 Cor. 5 and 6, 1 Tim. 5.

What are the keys?

The keys of the kingdom of heaven are the power or the ministry to loose and to bind, or to remit and retain sins. This ministry was instituted by Christ and was given to the Church. By it the minister of the Church, through the Word of the Gospel, announces in Christ's name the forgiveness of sins, the granting of the Holy Spirit and of eternal life to many and to individuals who are repentant and seeking pardon; and binds and excommunicates those who persevere in their sins securely and stubbornly.[13]

We observe that for both absolution and excommunication is it "the minister of the Gospel" who "bears witness in the name of Christ" and "announces in Christ's name"—not in the name of the bishop, district president or voters assembly—of the loosing or binding of sins. After all, the keys are "the ministry to loose and bind, or to remit or retain sins." Lest there be any doubt concerning the nature of the ministry—that it is a specific office, and not a general calling— Chytraeus further

13   David Chytraeus, *A Summary of the Christian Faith*, (Decatur, Illinois: Repristination Press, 1997) p. 134-5.

explained:

What is the ministry of the Gospel?

> The ministry of the Gospel is the office which God has instituted, the office of preaching and confessing the Word of God, the Law and the Gospel concerning Christ, in the public assembly of the Church; of rightly administering the sacraments; of announcing the forgiveness of sins or of absolving those who repent; of excommunicating the obstinate; and of ordaining ministers of the Church, through which ministry God is truly effective for the salvation of all who believe, Luke 24; Matt. 10, 18 and 28; Rom. 10; Eph. 4; 1 Tim. 5; 2 Tim. 2.[14]

Finally, Chytraeus included a comparison between two of the estates, the Church and the State. Listing the differences "between the ministry of the Gospel and political power," Chytraeus lists, "Third, they differ in *punishments*. The magistrate restrains and punishes the disobedient with physical force or the sword. The ministry of the Gospel reproves solely with the word or voice of the Law and with lawful excommunication."[15]

Martin Chemnitz makes the same points in his *Enchiridion*.[16] Chemnitz extolled the virtues of private absolution, and, as regards the impenitent, the responsibility of "the minister to use, not the loosing, bu the binding key against such people."[17] He observed regarding pastoral jurisdiction:

> But if ever in the ministry they bind and retain sins to the impenitent, according to the Word of God, with threat of divine wrath and curse, they should know that this is regarded as valid and certain also in heaven. In the same way, if they loose and forgive sins by proclaiming the grace of God to the penitent and believing, they should be sure that it is not only good words (as is commonly said), but that the same is also certain and confirmed in heaven (Mt. 16:19).

14   ibid., p. 144.
15   ibid., p. 145.
16   translated as *Ministry, Word, and Sacraments: An Enchiridion*, trans. by Luther Poellot (St. Louis: Concordia Publishing House, 1981).
17   ibid., p. 135.

Similarly the name keys should admonish the hearers not to despise the Word and ministry and regard it as a vain sound of words by which only the ears are struck, but that they might know and be firmly persuaded that if they want to enter the kingdom of heaven, the approach and entrance is not given and granted to them except through these keys.[18]

More witnesses could easily be evaluated to continue to emphasize these points, but time does not permit and the matters at hand have already been adequately established from the Lutheran Symbols themselves. Due diligence to study of the symbols amply reveals how far the LC—MS has fallen from the confessional understanding of pastoral responsibility.

Pastoral Responsibility and the Crisis in the LC—MS

A great deal of attention has rightly been given to the 'episcopal' power grab at the heart of 2004 Resolution 8-01A.[19] The decision to give district presidents indisputable authority as the final arbiters of all controversy in the Church is a naked repudiation of pastoral responsibility as set forth in the Lutheran Confessions. However, 8-01A is only the latest iteration of failed 'reconciliation' processes in the recent history of the synod. The spiritually bankrupt "win-win" system (which seemed institutionally oblivious to the reality of sin and the need for confession) was simply replaced by the "I-say-who-wins" system of the party which rules the synod.

How shall the confessional pastor respond to 8-01A? The previous 'reconciliation' process was, in the opinion of this presenter, already being abused to harass confessional pastors and interfere with pastoral responsibility. The new

18   ibid., p. 133.
19   The presenter has endeavored to deal with this resolution in two previous presentations: *Authority and Unity in the Church* and *"Here we have no Continuing City"* (both available at salemlutheranchurch.net).

system is even more open to such abuse for it makes the district presidents the decision makers concerning who will, or will not, face charges which could lead to expulsion from the synod. The presenter personally experienced how a district president imagined himself to be the final authority regarding the merits of a case of church discipline carried out within a congregation. With the broadly expanded authority of 8-01A, it may be anticipated that such papistical interference will only continue and grow far worse.

So how shall the confessional pastor respond to such tyranny? The pastor's responsibility before the Holy Trinity has not changed: he is still the one to whom the ministry of Word and Sacrament has been entrusted; he is still the one charged with the responsibility to bind and loose sins within the Church. The pastor must fulfill his office, therefore, regardless of how the rump bishops puff themselves up. This means one must be willing to suffer the abuse which they can dish out: a faithful pastor may find himself expelled from the synod for being faithful to his call. You will find that, at the end of the day, that doesn't hurt you anywhere near as much as they want it to. If you are expelled from the synod for faithfully fulfilling your office, it is true that the congregation where the Lord has called you to serve will face a choice. If you have been expelled from synod for faithfully serving the Lord in their midst, one would hope and pray that they would also be faithful. But what is the worst that could happen? That they would fail to be faithful, and remove you from your call *because* you were faithful in your calling? Better to have a clean conscience with regard to faithfully fulfilling your office than to prove one's self a hireling.

All confessional Lutheran pastors have taken an oath to the Holy Trinity to fulfill their ministries in accord with the Holy Scriptures and the Lutheran Confessions. It is the pastor who hears the charge given by inspiration of God through

St. Peter: "Shepherd the flock of God which is among you, serving as overseers, not by compulsion but willingly, not for dishonest gain but eagerly; not as being lords over those entrusted to you, but being examples to the flock; and when the Chief Shepherd appears, you will receive the crown of glory that does not fade away." (1 Pet. 5:2–4 NKJV)

Bishops, Councils and Authority in the Church In the Treatise on the Power and Primacy of the Pope

I.

From February 10 through March 6 of 1537, many of the theologians and civil authorities of the territories of the Smalcald League gathered in the city of Schmalkalden to consider a unified response to Pope Paul III's call for a Church Council. Martin Luther had been calling for such a council for nearly 20 years, for there was a need to address the division which had occurred within the Church. Nevertheless, the decision to actually convene a council caught the Lutherans somewhat less that fully prepared. The pope scheduled the council to begin on May 8th, 1537, at Mantua in Italy. Following the counsel of the Wittenberg theologians, John Frederick, the elector of Saxony, had come to the conclusion that he would attend the council, and thus the Lutherans understood the necessity of reaffirming their unity.[1]

The Smalcald League was organized in 1535 at the Diet of Smalcald as a confessional Lutheran alliance. At that time, it was agreed that the members of the League should promise "to provide for such teaching and preaching as was in harmony with the Word of God and the pure teaching of our [Augsburg] Confession."[2] Indeed, Bente observes that "Membership in the Smalcald League was conditioned on accepting the Apology [of the Augsburg Confession] as well as

---

1   J. L. Neve., *Introduction to Lutheran Symbolics*, (Repristination Press: Fort Wayne, 1995) p. 339–340.
2   F. Bente, *Historical Introductions to the Book of Concord*, (Concordia Publishing House: St. Louis, 1965) p. 9.

the Augustana. Both were also subscribed to in the *Wittenberg Concord* of 1536."[3] This final observation is of particular significance, for one must appreciate the importance of the Wittenberg Concord to understanding the decisions which were made at Schmalkalden in 1537.

In May 1536, Luther and the Wittenberg theologians had come to doctrinal agreement with Martin Bucer and Wolfgang Capito, two of the key Strasbourg theologians among those whom we would call the 'Reformed,' and confessed a common teaching regarding the Lord's Supper in the Wittenberg Concord. It was after that agreement had been accomplished that John Frederick commissioned Luther to draft the document which we now know as the Smalcald Articles; the bull convoking the council was issued on June 4, 1536 and on December 11 John Frederick commissioned Luther.[4] The articles were duly drawn up by Luther and "having been submitted to approved by his colleagues, Justus Jonas, Cruciger, Bugenhagen and Melanchthon, and by Amsdorf, Agricola and Spalatin, who had been summoned to Wittenberg, were sent to the elector January 3. "[5] Neve states that "It was the elector's wish that here [at Schmalkalden in 1537] the articles of Luther should be adopted by the whole convention as another confessional document of the Lutheran Church. But his plan did not work."[6] The reason why this plan did not work seems quite simple: Luther's statements in the Smalcald Articles concerning the Lord's Supper did not conform to the language of the Wittenberg Concord. In the assessment of J. L. Neve:

> And indeed, a comparison with Luther's autograph edition (by Zangemeister) shows that Luther had first written in entire consonance with the Wittenberg Concord: "that under

---

3   ibid., p. 47.
4   ibid.; see also Neve, p. 340, and Jacobs, H. E., *The Book of Concord*, 2 vols., (The Johann Gerhard Institute: Decatur, 1996) vol. 2, p. 42.
5   Jacobs 2:42.
6   Neve, p. 342.

bread and wine there be the true body and blood of Christ in the Supper". But this he crossed out and wrote: "that bread and wine in the Supper are the true body and blood of Christ".[7]

Philip of Hesse prevailed upon the princes to remain with the Augsburg Confession and the confession which had been expressed in the Wittenberg Concord the previous year. This argument was probably made even more appealing by the fact that Martin Bucer was among those in attendance at Schmalkalden. Thus Luther's articles were not officially adopted, and the princes also came to the agreement that they would not attend the pope's council. Since the pope had declared in September of 1536 that the purpose of the council would be "the utter extirpation of the poisonous, pestilential Lutheran heresy"[8] it seemed utterly pointless (even self-destructive) to attend the council.

However, the princes did agree on two points: "(1) The theologians should once more go over the Augsburg Confession and establish it with new arguments from Scripture and the Fathers in such a way that there be no conflict with the Wittenberg Concord. (2) *Something special should be drawn up with regard to the papacy*, because this had been left undone at Augsburg for the purpose of not displeasing the emperor."[9] Clearly the first goal was not accomplished at Schmalkalden ("because of lack of books and time," Neve observes)[10], but

---

7   ibid. Luther had co-authored the Concord with Capito and Bucer. Following the agreement, all three joined in receiving the Sacrament together—certainly a sign of wholehearted commitment on the part of Luther! Jacobs observes: "Melanchthon from the very beginning was averse to the negotiations, and writes on the day the Concord was signed that he had no hope of any permanent good" (Jacobs 2:284). History has proven that Melanchthon's 'pessimism' was well-warranted.

8   Bente, p. 47.

9   Neve, p. 343. Italics in original.

10   P. 344. The first article of the Wittenberg Concord states: "We confess that, according to the words of Irenaeus, the Eucharist consists of two things, an earthly and a heavenly. They hold and teach, therefore, that with the bread and

Melanchthon endeavored to address the second point, finishing his *Tractatus de potestate et primatu papae* on February 17.[11] The Smalcald League's formal subscription to the Treatise probably took place on February 24th or 25th. The importance of the Treatise as a confessional document should not be understated. Rather, as H. E. Jacobs explains:

> The symbolical authority of the Appendix not only rests upon the same ground as that of the Smalcald Articles proper, but it possesses a more undisputed claim for its immediate acceptance as confessional from the fact that, with the Augsburg Confession and the Apology, it was expressly mentioned and approved over their signatures by the princes and estates in the recess of the conference. For the time the Appendix possessed a higher importance than the Smalcald Articles themselves, as the latter were composed with reference to an event which it was now manifest would not occur, while the former had in view the new relations and circumstances in which the Lutheran princes and estates were placed by their refusal of the offer of a general council.[12]

Much has been said and written regarding Melanchthon's 'qualified' subscription to the Smalcald Articles: "But of the Pope, I hold that if he would allow the Gospel, for the sake of the peace and general unity of Christians, who are now under him, and may be under him hereafter, the superiority over bishops which he has in other respects could be allowed to him, according to human right, also by us."[13] How are we to understand Melanchthon's subscription? Russell focused on Melanchthon's concerns regarding the dangers of the princes serving as 'emergency bishops':

wine the body and blood of Christ are truly and substantially present, offered and received." (Jacobs, vol. 2, 285) It is possible that Melanchthon believed he was fulfilling the intention of the Smalcald League when in 1540 he changed Augustana X in his Variata edition to read: "Of the Lord's Supper they teach that, together with the bread and wine, the body and blood of Christ are truly tendered to those who eat in the Lord's Supper." (ibid., 139)

11   Neve, p. 344.
12   Jacobs 2:45.
13   Jacobs 1:377.

A second important datum to keep in mind in order to understand Melanchthon's subscription to SA [the Smalcald Articles] is to recognize that he had been concerned for some time about the possible domination of the church by the princes if episcopal authority (which was derived from the primacy of the bishop of Rome) were completely abandoned. In fact, Melanchthon had originally desired that AC be subscribed only by the theologians and not the princes, so as to underscore the theological (as opposed to the political) nature of the matters involved. This concern is evident when, from Augsburg on August 31, 1530, Melanchthon wrote to Joachim Camerarius:

Oh would that it would be possible, not indeed to confirm the despotism, but restore the administration of the bishops. For I envision what kind of church we shall have when ecclesiastical polity is dissolved. I see that afterwards there will arise a much more intolerable tyranny [of the princes] than there ever was.[14]

In light of the later history of the Church, Melanchthon certainly had good reason to be concerned regarding the state churches. But Russell's claim that episcopal authority "was derived from the primacy of the bishop of Rome" is certainly not a view which can be credibly attributed to Melanchthon. Thus we come to the subject at hand: bishops and church councils and authority in the Church. In the Treatise on the Power and Primacy of the Pope we have, if you will, a conclusion of the Evangelical Lutheran Church's confession regarding the authority of the bishops—a confession begun in the articles of the *Augustana* and its Apology.

II.

The structure of the Treatise is fairly straight forward, being divided into two parts, the first part then being subdi-

---

14   Russell, William R., *Luther's Theological Testament*, (Fortress Press: Minneapolis, 1995), p. 53–54.

vided into three articles.[15] The first part deals with the papal contention concerning three points:

1. "The Roman pontiff claims for himself that by divine right he is above all bishops and pastors" (§1);

2. "he adds also that by divine right he has both swords, i.e. the right of bestowing and transferring kingdoms" (§2);

3. "he says that to believe this is necessary to salvation." (§3)

The Treatise denounces all of these papal claims in the strongest terms: "These three articles we hold to be false, godless, tyrannical and pernicious to the Church." (§4) Such claims are, first of all, refuted "from the Gospel": "we will show from the Gospel that the Roman bishop is not by divine right above other bishops and pastors." (§7) Indeed, the Treatise refutes the papal claim of primacy from the testimony of Scripture, Church history, and through the negation of the papal arguments in favor of such a primacy. However, the central argument throughout the entire Treatise could be summarized as follows: 'All those who called to the office of the holy ministry (be they bishops or pastors) have a common calling and office.' The beginning of the second part of the Treatise states this point explicitly:

> The Gospel has assigned to those who preside over churches the command to teach the Gospel, to remit sins, to administer the sacraments, and besides jurisdiction, viz. the command to excommunicate those whose crimes are known, and again of absolving the repenting.
>
> And by the confession of all, even of the adversaries, it is clear that this power by divine right is common to all who preside over churches, whether they be called pastors, or presbyters, or bishops. (§§ 60–61)

These same responsibilities were enumerated in Article XXVIII of the Augsburg Confession and the Apology as the

---

15 A thorough outline is provided in Appendix 1.

"power of the Keys, or the power of the bishops".[16] Even in 1530, however, the *Augustana* clearly confessed that such responsibilities were "the ministry of the Word and Sacraments" (§ 9, §21)—and thus were not limited to those who were called 'bishops' according to the common usage of the period—and the confessors clearly delineated that "it is lawful for bishops or pastors to make ordinances that things be done orderly in the Church" (§ 53)—a clear implication that the ministry was one office, even if divided into various grades.

Although *jure divino*, the Lutheran Confessions maintain the unity of the one office, nevertheless there was a clear emphasis in both the *Augustana* and the Apology regarding the earnest desire on the part of the Lutherans to maintain the grades of office *jure humano*, even under Roman bishops—if they would allow the Gospel 'free course.' Thus it is taught in the *Augustana*: "But the bishops might easily retain the lawful obedience of the people, if they would not insist upon the observance of such traditions as cannot be kept with a good conscience," (XVIII:69) and "Now it is not our design to wrest the government from the bishops, but this one thing is asked, namely, that they allow the Gospel to be purely taught, and that they relax some few observances which cannot be kept without sin." (§77)

---

16   "But this is their opinion, that the power of the Keys, or the power of the bishops, according to the Gospel, is a power or commandment of God, to preach the Gospel, to remit and retain sins, and to administer sacraments. For with that commandment, Christ sends forth His Apostles [John 20:21 sqq.]: 'As My Father has sent Me, even so send I you. Receive ye the Holy Ghost. Whosesoever sins ye remit, they are remitted unto them; and whosesoever sins ye retain, they are retained.' [Mark 16:15]: 'Go, preach the Gospel to every creature.'" (AC XXVIII: 5–7) "But we are speaking of a bishop according to the Gospel. And the ancient division of power into 'power of the order' and 'power of jurisdiction' is pleasing to us. Therefore the bishop has the power of the order, i.e. the ministry of the Word and Sacraments; he has also the power of jurisdiction, i.e. the authority to excommunicate those guilty of open crimes, and again to absolve them if they are converted and seek absolution." (AP XXVIII:13)

The Apology also emphasizes the desire to maintain the present ecclesiastical order: "Concerning this subject, we have frequently testified in this assembly that it is our greatest wish to maintain Church polity and the grades in the Church, even though they have been made by human authority..." (AP XIV:24) That the Lutherans were departing from such Church polity was not due to any rebellion on the part of the confessors; rather, it was because the bishops "put to death the poor innocent men." (§25) "Thus the cruelty of the bishops is the reason why that canonical government, which we greatly desired to maintain, is in some places dissolved." (§25)

It should be noted that the refutation of the second claim of the papists ("...that by divine right he has both swords..." [§2]) is an extension of the argument presented in *Augustana* XXVIII:

> This power [of the keys or of the bishops] is exercised only by teaching or preaching the Gospel and administering the sacraments, according to the calling, either to many or to individuals. ... Therefore, since the power of the Church grants eternal things, and is exercised only by the ministry of the Word, it does not interfere with civil government; no more than the art of singing interferes with civil government. For civil government deals with other things than does the Gospel; the civil rulers defend not souls, but bodies and bodily things against manifest injuries, and restrain men with the sword and bodily punishments in order to preserve civil justice and peace.
>
> Therefore the power of the Church and the civil power must not be confounded. The power of the Church has its own commission, to teach the Gospel and to administer the sacraments. Let it not break into the office of another; let it not transfer the kingdoms of this world; let it not abrogate the laws of civil rulers; let it not abolish lawful obedience; let it not interfere with judgments concerning civil ordinances or contracts; let it not prescribe laws to civil rulers concerning the form of the Commonwealth. (§§ 8, 10–13)

Thus it was concluded: "If bishops have any power of the sword, that power they have, not as bishops, by the commission of the Gospel, but by human law, having received it of Kings and Emperors, for the civil administration of what is theirs. This, however, is another office than the ministry of the Gospel." (AC XXVIII:19) Given that this point receives such thorough treatment in the *Augustana*, it is readily understandable that the second article is the shortest portion of the first part of the Treatise: having established that all bishops are equal in office before the Lord, that which pertains to all bishops regarding secular authority will apply to the bishop of Rome, as well.

In the Treatise, it is the equality (*jure divino*) of all those serving in the holy office which reduces the pope to one bishop among many, and then the bishops to being one grade within the one office of the ministry. The entire argument against the supremacy of the Roman pontiff is based in the equality of the apostles. Christ's prohibition of lordship among the apostles (Luke 22:25), the call of the apostles following our Lord's resurrection (John 20:21), and St. Paul's assertion that he was neither ordained nor confirmed by St. Peter (Gal. 2:7sq.) are the primary *sedes doctrinae* asserted for this equality. Melanchthon then argues that Paul "teaches that the authority of the ministry depends upon the Word of God, and that Peter was not superior to the other apostles, and that ordination or confirmation ws not to be sought from Peter alone." (§10) The Treatise then contends on the basis of 1 Cor. 3:6 that this equality extends not just within the apostolate, but throughout the office of the ministry: "In 1 Cor. 3:6, Paul makes ministers equal, and teaches that the Church is above the ministers. Hence superiority or lordship over the Church or the rest of the ministers is not ascribed to Peter. ... Paul removes this pretext from Peter, and denies that his authority is to be preferred to the rest or to the Church." (§ 11)

Melanchthon's assertion that "the Church is above the ministers" has been a source of confusion. It is vital, therefore, that we remember the context of this statement. The Treatise was written in the context of the anticipated church council; Melanchthon continues in the next paragraph (§12) to observe

> Hence it was first by human law, i.e. the resolution of the Council [of Nicaea], that the authority of the Roman bishop arose. If already by divine law the Roman bishop would have had superiority, it would not have been lawful for the Council to have removed any right from him and to have transferred it to the bishop of Alexandria; yea all the bishops of the East ought perpetually to have sought ordination and confirmation from the bishop of Rome.

The point made in §11 thus concerns *conciliar*, not *congregational*, authority. Again, Melanchthon asserted in § 56: "But since the decisions of Synods are the decisions of the Church, and not of the Popes, it is especially incumbent on kings to check the license of the popes, and to so act that the power of judging and decreeing from the Word of God be not wrested from the Church." It was often the contention of the Lutherans that it was the responsibility of the secular authorities (e.g. the king, emperor, etc.) to convene councils, at which the bishops would then discuss the matter under contention, and render their decisions according to God's Word.[17]

In § 49, the Treatise contends that one of the "great sins" of the pope is that "he appropriates the decision of the Church, and does not permit ecclesiastical controversies to be judged according to the prescribed mode; yea, he contends that he is above the Council, and that the decrees of Councils can be rescinded, just as the canons sometimes impudently speak." Thus we see that the clear language of the Treatise is that the "prescribed mode" for a "decision of the Church" concerning "ecclesiastical controversies" is the church council.

---

17   See, for example, Luther's *On the Councils and the Church* (1539) and Melanchthon's *The Church and the Authority of the Word* (1539).

The influence of prominent conciliarists such as Jean Gerson (1363–1429) can be seen throughout the Book of Concord.[18] Certainly the Lutheran assertion that church council contained a certain lay and episcopal authority (as they were to be convened by the civil authorities, and their decrees determined by the bishops) contains some echo of Marsiglio of Padua's (1275–1342) contentions in his *Defensor Pacis*. But the Lutheran fathers did not attribute infallibility to the councils any more than they would have yielded to the pope's claim to such authority. They certainly did not see an ecumenical council as necessary for those churches which were already reformed. As Luther observed in the preface to the Smalcald Articles:

> I sincerely desire to see a truly Christian Council, whereby yet many matters and persons would be helped. Not that we need it, for our churches are now, through God's grace, so illumined and cared for by the pure Word and right use of the sacraments, by knowledge of the various callings and of right works, that we on our part ask for no Council, and on such points have nothing better to hope or expect from a Council; but because we see in the bishoprics everywhere so many parishes vacant and desolate that one's heart would break. (§ 10)

In fact, Luther and Melanchthon both went to great lengths in the 1539 writings on the church councils to point out that the councils *could* and *did* err. Thus Melanchthon wrote: "Although the true church, which is small, retains the articles of faith, nevertheless this same true church can possess errors which obscure the articles of faith."[19] Again:

> I say the same thing about the synods: The synods of the church which, while disputing about the Word of God,

---

18   Luther actually cites Gerson as an example of the efficacy of the baptism of infants, declaring in the Large Catechism: "But since God confirms baptism by the gift of His Holy Ghost, as is plainly perceptible in some of the Church Fathers, as St. Bernard, Gerson, John Huss, and others, who were baptized in infancy..." (LC IV:50)

19   Melanchthon, Philip, "The Church and the Authority of the Word (1539)," in *Melanchthon—Selected Writings*, trans. by Charles Leander Hill, (Augsburg Publishing House: Minneapolis, 1962) p. 140.

do teach and admonish us, are to be heard. But let judgment be used and when they yield us things that are true, let us believe them because of the Word of God. For example, the Synod of Nicea piously and usefully taught and admonished all posterity about the Son of God, but we believe the article, not because of the synod, but because we see it has been so transmitted in the Word of God.

Other things which are outside of the Scriptures are not to be so embraced, such as when the Synod of Nicea instituted the canons of penance, which are human traditions outside of the Scriptures and have been the seeds for a multitude of superstitious opinions.[20]

Luther illustrates the same point from the example of Nicaea: "This council decreed, among other things, that apostate Christians shall be readmitted, for seven years of penance. If they died in the meantime, they were to be absolved and not denied the sacrament; today's council-screamers do not keep this, but transgress it and consign the dying Christians to purgatory, thus giving them more penance."[21] And Luther observed that the council's decrees were being exploited by false teachers in his own time: "But in the Council of Nicaea is clearly written the article that one should rebaptize the heretics, the Paulianists or Photinians. ... Thus Anabaptism tries to justify itself against St. Augustine and us all, because the Nicene council and other earlier councils and fathers agreed with Cyprian."[22] Thus decrees neither of popes nor councils could establish doctrine; neither were they to be trusted as free from error:

However, while we both [orthodox and heterodox] thus cull from the councils and the fathers, they what they like and we what we like, and cannot reach an agreement—because the fathers themselves disagree as much as do the councils—who, my dear man, is going to preach to the poor souls who

20   ibid., p. 144.
21   Luther, Martin, "On the Councils and the Church," in *Luther's Works* (Fortress Press: Philadelphia, 1966) p. 33.
22   ibid., p. 44–45.

know nothing of such culling and quarreling? Is that tending the sheep of Christ, when we ourselves do not know whether what we are feeding them is grass or poison, hay or dung? And are they to dangle and hang until it is settled and the council arrives at a decision? Oh, how poorly Christ would have provided for the church if this is how things have to go on! No, there must be another way than proving things by means of councils and fathers, or there could have been no church since the days of the apostles—which is impossible, for it is written, "I believe one holy, Christians church," and "I am with you always, to the close of the age" [Matt. 28:20]. These words must be the truth, even if all the fathers and councils were wrong! The Man must be called "I am the truth" [John 14:6]; fathers and councils should on the other hand be called "Every man is a liar" [Rom. 3:4] whenever they contradict each other.[23]

The point which Luther and Melanchthon are contending for must be clearly understood: it is *not* that they are dismissive of the legacy bequeathed to the church in the writings of the fathers and the decrees of the councils; rather, they are simply maintaining that the Church should always submit to the Word of the Lord of the Church because human authority (the councils and the fathers) *could* and *did* err. As Melanchthon observed:

> It is a very frequent custom to contend as to just how much weight is to be attributed to the opinions of the church, the decrees of the synods, and the sayings of the Scriptures. For although we do indeed embrace the Word of God, nevertheless, since there seem to be ambiguous passages in apostolic writings, some contend that the opinions of the church are to be followed rather than the writings of the apostles.
>
> Then they add the false claim that the authority of the church is to be preferred to the Word of God and that the church can alter things which have been handed down in the Word of God. As proof of these opinions they quote a passage of Augustine: "I would not believe the Gospel unless

23   ibid., p. 47–48.

the authority of the church moved me to it." Accordingly, under the false pretext of the name of the church, the pontiffs decide and teach in accordance with their own desire many things contrary to the Word of God and confirm and establish false doctrine and false practices. And it is solely the name of the church that is keeping very many persons even now from the true doctrine of the Gospel which we profess. Therefore it is necessary to warn people in a correct manner about the authority of the church.

On the other hand, there are some rather impudent characters who, when weaving new opinions from scriptural sayings which have been grossly distorted, absolutely reject the unanimity of the true church and all of the synods without discrimination. An example is Servetus when he opposes the church of all ages, perverts the statements about the Word in John 1, and seeks after, as he himself thinks, a more elegant interpretation. Therefore, that such impudence be repressed in some manner by walls, so to speak, is a task of the church, just as the ancient synods and writers adduce the primary testimonies accepted by the apostles and certain authors.[24]

Thus, neither popes nor the bishops (as they are heard through the voice of the councils) are to be heard or obeyed if what they teach or command is contrary to the Word of God. Thus it is declared in the Treatise: "But since by divine authority the grades of bishop and pastor are not diverse, it is manifest that ordination by a pastor in his own church has been appointed by divine law. Therefore when the regular bishops become enemies of the Church, or are unwilling to administer ordination, the churches retain their own right." (§§ 65–66) The Church shall not be deprived of the ministry which the Lord of the Church has established to feed and nourish her (AC V). The Lutheran fathers were hesitant to break with the established canonical polity; it could readily be maintained that they should have done more in Germany to maintain that polity, in service of the Gospel (as was done in Scandinavia).

---

24   Melanchthon, p. 133–134.

But the teaching of the Treatise, although it does set forth the situation of the Church in a time of severe deprivation, is nevertheless a clearly biblical teaching. They clearly confessed that the gates of Hades would not prevail against the Church; the ministry of the Gospel would be sustained:

> As to the declaration: "Upon this rock I will build My Church," certainly the Church has not been built upon the authority of man, but upon the ministry of the confession which Peter made, in which he proclaims that Jesus is the Christ, the Son of God. He accordingly addresses him as a minister: "Upon this rock," i.e. upon this ministry. Furthermore, the ministry of the New Testament is not bound to persons and places, as the Levitical ministry, but is is dispersed throughout the whole world, and is there where God gives His gifts, apostles, prophets, pastors, teachers; neither does this ministry avail on account of the authority of any person, but on account of the Word given by Christ. (Treatise §§ 25–26)

Appendix 1.

Structural outline of the Treatise on the Power and Primacy of the Pope from volume 2 of the H. E. Jacobs edition of the Book of Concord.

I. Of the Pope, §1–59

Introduction: The Points in controversy stated, §§1–6.

1. The bishop of Rome not universal bishop according to divine right—

    (a) Proved from Scripture, §§7–11.

    (b) From the testimony of the ancient Church, §§12–21.

    (c) Scripture passages cited to the contrary explained, §§ 22–30.

2. The power conferred by Christ upon His apostles purely spiritual, §§ 31–34.

3. The necessity of complete severance from the government of the Pope, §§ 35–59.

    (a) No obedience to be rendered those who defend godless services or false doctrine, § 38.

    (b) The Popes defend such services and doctrines, §§ 39–48.

        (aa) The marks of Antichrist applied to the Papacy, §§ 39–42.

        (bb) Some of the godless services and false doctrines enumerated: the profanation of masses, the Romish doctrines of repentance, of justification, of sin, of the necessity of the enumeration of sins, of satisfactions, indulgences, worship of saints, the tradition concerning celibacy, the false doctrine and godless service of vows, §§ 43–48.

    (c) The two great sins of the Papacy: of defending these errors by unjust punishments, and of wresting the decision of ecclesiastical controversies from the Church, §§ 49–51.

(d) An appeal to all godly men, and especially to rulers, to reject these errors, and to provide for their removal from the Church, §§52-59.

II. Of the Power and Jurisdiction of Bishops, §§ 60–82

1. The parity, according to divine right, of all pastors, presbyters and bishops, §§60–64.

2. The consequent legitimacy, according to divine right, of ordination performed by a pastor in his own church, and the necessity for the Church to assert this right when the regular bishops are enemies of the Gospel, §§ 65–72.

3. For the same reason, the jurisdiction of excommunication is denied the bishops, and transferred to the pastors, §§ 73–76.

4. The jurisdiction in forensic cases, especially those pertaining to marriage, having been committed to them entirely on the authority of human right, should also, because of its unjust exercise, be withdrawn, §§ 77, 78.

5. Summing up of the argument of the Appendix, showing the reasons why they are no longer to be recognized as bishops, § 79.

6. The charge added that the bishops are defrauding the Church of alms, §§ 80–82.

THE FUTURE OF ECCLESIASTICAL OVERSIGHT AMONG CONFESSIONAL LUTHERANS

Introduction

I have been assigned the topic, "The Future of Ecclesiastical Oversight among Confessional Lutherans." Several points which are implicit in this title deserve to be drawn out from the beginning of this presentation. The title implies that there *has been* ecclesiastical oversight among confessional Lutherans in the past, and perhaps even in the present, and that the *future* of such oversight is worthy of consideration. The title also implies that confessional Lutherans have a future in which to be overseen, which may seem, in the minds of some, a less than certain thing. While certainly no special promise is attached to the name "Lutheran" (and, indeed, adherents of the Unaltered Augsburg Confession have periodically expressed reticence about describing themselves with such a schismatic-sounding epithet), nevertheless we believe, teach and confess, "that one holy Church is to continue forever. The Church is the congregation of saints, in which the Gospel is rightly taught and the Sacraments rightly administered." (AC VII:1) The Book of Concord, being the faithful exposition of the doctrine of Holy Scripture, it is an article of faith that the only holy Church, which continues forever, will be that congregation of saints in which that doctrine is rightly taught and the Sacraments rightly administered. Neither arguments from antiquity (the argument of Rome, the Eastern Orthodox, and smaller schismatic, 'old catholic' groups) nor contemporaneity (and here we think primarily of those who believe *vox populi vox dei*) are sufficient of themselves to establish the Church; we seek to uphold the confessional, and thus scriptural, teaching and practices of the one, holy, catholic and apostolic Church.

We are concerned for the future of ecclesiastical oversight because it is a scriptural and confessional concern. St. Paul wrote in his first Epistle to St. Timothy, "This is a faithful saying: If a man desires the position of a bishop, he desires a good work." (1 Tim. 3:1) Some may be inclined to question the 'episcopal' orientation of this presentation; but in this regard we plead the very definition of the words under consideration. Oversight is conducted by an overseer, which is, in the language of Holy Scripture, an *episcopos*. We shall thus consider the nature of such oversight, both as it exists within the congregation, and as it exists within a larger fellowship of those to whom Christ has entrusted the office of the keys.

There are so many topics—dogmatic and historical—which come together under our consideration today that I must apologize in advance for a presentation which must, of necessity, perhaps seem somewhat fragmentary. Nevertheless, it is my hope that by the time of our conclusion the threads will have woven together.

Episcopos and Episcopé in the Holy Scriptures

The words επισκοπεω ("oversee, care for"), επισκοπη ("visitation") and επισκοπος ("overseer") are the most immediately relevant terms for our discussion today if we are to address 'ecclesiastical oversight' in biblical terms, and we find these key terms being used in both the LXX and the New Testament.

In the LXX, we read that the Lord oversees the land; thus we read in Deuteronomy 11 that it is "a land for which the LORD your God cares; the eyes of the LORD your God are always on it, from the beginning of the year to the very end of the year." (v. 12)[1] He also visits His people as a Shepherd: "For the idols speak delusion; the diviners envision lies; and tell false dreams; they comfort in vain. Therefore the people

---

1   "γη, ην κυριος ο θεος σου επισκοπειται αυτην,..."

wend their way like sheep; they are in trouble because there is no shepherd. My anger is kindled against the shepherds, and I will punish the goatherds. For the LORD of hosts will visit [επισκεψομαι] His flock, the house of Judah, and will make them as His royal horse in the battle." (Zech. 10:2–3) As the shepherds had led the people astray, the Lord visits His people as the overseeing Shepherd. The Lord Himself is described as *episcopos* in Job 20:29. As the *Theological Dictionary of the New Testament* observes, "The LXX calls God *episkopos* in Job 20:29 with a clear reference to his judicial function." (p. 246)

The LXX also uses επισκοπεω with regard to divinely-appointed overseers. Thus we read in Numbers 27 that Moses said to the LORD: "Let the LORD, the God of the spirits of all flesh, set a man over the congregation, who may go out before them and go in before them, who may lead them out and bring them in, that the congregation of the LORD may not be like sheep which have no shepherd." (v. 16–17)[2] "And the LORD said to Moses: 'Take Joshua the son of Nun with you, a man in whom is the Spirit, and lay your hand on him; set him before Eleazar the priest and before all the congregation, and inaugurate him in their sight.' And you shall give some of your authority to him, that all the congregation of the children of Israel may be obedient." (Num. 27:18–20)

Undeniably, the Lord gave commandment to Moses to ordain Joshua as an overseer who had a share in the authority of Moses over the people of Israel, and that the role of Joshua as an overseer was to serve the congregation so that they would not be "like sheep which have no shepherd." A connection seems readily apparent between Moses' ordination of Joshua and Christ's call to His twelve disciples, for St. Matthew thus wrote: "Then Jesus went about all the cities and villages, teaching in their synagogues, preaching the gospel

---

2   "Επισκεψασθω κυριος ο θεος ... ανθρωπον επι της συναγωγης ταυτης..."

of the kingdom, and healing every sickness and every disease among the people. But when He saw the multitudes, He was moved with compassion for them, because they were weary and scattered, like sheep having no shepherd. Then He said to His disciples, 'The harvest truly is plentiful, but the laborers are few. Therefore pray the Lord of the harvest to send out laborers into His harvest.' And when He had called His twelve disciples to Him, He gave them power over unclean spirits, to cast them out, and to heal all kinds of sickness, and all kinds of disease." (Mat. 9:35–10:1) In both circumstances, the concern is that the people would be left as sheep without a shepherd, and the Lord causes those who are to overseer the flock to be sent with the authority of the One who sent them.

In the LXX, Επισκοπος is used to refer to an office, or area of responsibility in which one serves. Thus the επισκοπος Ελεαζαρ υιος Ααρων του ιερεως—"the appointed duty of Eleazar the son of Aaron the priest"—was "the oil for the light, the sweet incense, the daily grain offering, the anointing oil, the oversight [η επισκοπη] of all the tabernacle, of all that is in it, with the sanctuary and its furnishings." (Num. 4:16) Zebul was the officer [επισκοπος] of Shechem (Judges 9:28). Also, when the temple was restored and repaired under Hilkiah the high priest, we are told "the men did the work faithfully. Their overseers [επισκοποι] were Jahath and Obadiah the Levites, of the sons of Merari, and Zechariah and Meshullam, of the sons of the Kohathites, to supervise [επισκοπειν]." (2 Chron. 34:12) We read in 2 Kings 11 that under Jehoiada the priest, before the time when Jehoash ordered the repair of the temple, "And all the people of the land went to the temple of Baal, and tore it down. They thoroughly broke in pieces its altars and images, and killed Mattan the priest of Baal before the altars. And the priest appointed officers [επισκοπους] over the house of the LORD." (v. 18)

David makes use of the word επισκοπη in the sense

of a specific office in Psalm 109 when he wrote of the wicked man: "Let his days be few, and let another take his office."[3] St. Peter picks up on David's use of the term επισκοπη, and specifically connects David's use of this word as prophetic, relating it directly to the apostolic ministry, as he discusses the vacancy left in the apostolate after the treachery and death of Judas: "For it is written in the book of Psalms: 'Let his dwelling place be desolate, and let no one live in it'; and 'Let another take his office'" (Acts 1:20).[4]

Given the LXX precedents regarding the use of επισκοπη and related terms, we must certainly consider the weight attached to the term in New Testament usage. St. Peter spoke of Judas as one who had "a part in this ministry [τον κληρον της διακονιας ταυτης]"—a ministry which is specifically an office [επισκοπη]. (Acts 1:17, 20) To have a share in the ministry of the apostles is to occupy the apostolic office.

Just as the Lord is referred to as *Episcopos* in the Old Testament, so St. Peter declares in 1 Peter 2: "For you were like sheep going astray, but have now returned to the Shepherd and Overseer [τον ποιμενα και επισκοπον] of your souls." (v. 25) As in the LXX, the linkage is made between shepherding and overseeing— and this connection is carried over to those whom the Lord calls as presbyters over His flock. Thus St. Peter declares in the fifth chapter of the same epistle:

> The elders [πρεσβυτερους] who are among you I exhort, I who am a fellow elder [συμπρεσβυτερος] and a witness of the sufferings of Christ, and also a partaker of the glory that will be revealed: Shepherd [ποιμανατε] the flock of God which is among you, serving as overseers [επισκοπουντες], not by compulsion but willingly, not for dishonest gain but eagerly; nor as being lords over those entrusted to you, but

---

3   "γενηθητωσαν αι ημεραι αυτου ολιγαι, και την επισκοπην αυτου λαβοι ετερπος"

4   Please note: the KJV translates επισκοπη here as "bishopric," as does Luther in his German translation: "... und sein Bisthum empfahe ein anderer."

being examples to the flock; and when the Chief Shepherd appears, you will receive the crown of glory that does not fade away. (5:1–4)

Thus St. Peter understands that as Christ Jesus is Shepherd and Bishop, so the presbyters (among whom he counts himself) are both shepherds and bishops.

St. Paul also links the presbyterate and episcopate, apparently using the two terms to refer to one office, as he wrote to St. Titus, "For this reason I left you in Crete, that you should set in order the things that are lacking, and appoint elders in every city as I commanded you," (1:5) and then continues to speak of that office as that of bishop: "For a bishop must be blameless, as a steward of God, not self-willed, not quick-tempered, not given to wine, not violent, not greedy for money, but hospitable, a lover of what is good, sober-minded, just, holy, self-controlled, holding fast the faithful word as he has been taught, that he may be able, by sound doctrine, both to exhort and convict those who contradict." (1:7–9) Paul emphasized vocation of overseer as an office as he wrote to the Philippians, "To all the saints in Christ Jesus who are in Philippi, with the bishops and deacons" and to St. Timothy, "This is a faithful saying: If a man desires the position of a bishop, he desires a good work." (1 Tim. 3:1)

In Acts 20, as St. Paul traveled toward Jerusalem, "he sent to Ephesus and called for the elders of the church [πρεσβ–υτερους της εκκλησιας]," (v. 17) and then addressed them, in part, with the words: "Therefore take heed to yourselves and to all the flock, among which the Holy Spirit has made you overseers [επισκοπους], to shepherd [ποιμαινειν] the church of God, which He purchased with His own blood." (v. 28) Thus we see that both St. Peter and St. Paul describe the work of the presbyters/bishops as that of shepherding the flock, a role which is evocative of the call of Joshua, and as a ministry of which the holy apostles are a part as "fellow presbyters." In terms of the teaching of the New Testament, the office of the holy ministry, *iure divino*, is one office, and the incumbents of that office are variously described as "presbyter," "bishop," "shepherd," and other titles, as well as by other descriptive terms, such as "stewards of the mysteries of God." It is crucial to our understanding of "ecclesiastical oversight" that when we speak of such "overseers" in the scriptural sense, we speak of all ministers of the Gospel as they oversee the flocks which Christ Jesus has entrusted to their care. It is also important to understand that the term "elder" in the New Testament refers to the office of the holy ministry; it is not to be confused with the modern innovation (borrowed from the Presbyterians) of so-called 'lay elders' in the congregation.

We shall soon turn to an examination of the Book of Concord's teaching regarding ecclesiastical oversight, but before doing so, it is worth noting, in passing, the developments which appear to have taken place immediately after the generation of the apostles, if not directly under their supervision. It has been repeatedly observed that by the time of death of St. Ignatius of Antioch (ca. 98–117 A.D.), the office of the ministry had already developed into a 'monarchial episcopacy.' Thus, for example, Hans von Campenhausen wrote in *Ecclesiastical Authority and Spiritual Power in the Church of the First Three Centuries*:

> In the period between Clement and Hermas, a fundamentally new picture is presented by the letters of Ignatius, Bishop of Antioch, written on his last journey, which took him to Rome as a martyr. They reveal an advanced stage of developed hierarchical order, which is connected with the fact that they are of Syrian provenance, and possible also with the particular circumstances of life in the metropolis of Antioch. In Ignatius a system of monarchical episcopacy has already been implemented, so that all important functions are in the hands of the one bishop. The clergy itself no longer constitutes a single group of 'reverend' and 'leading' men over against the rest of

the congregation, but is sharply divided into grades.[5] (p. 97)

As regards the 'monarchial episcopacy,' Ignatius' words to the Smyrnaeans are perhaps most famous:

8. You must all follow the lead of the bishop, as Jesus Christ followed that of the Father; follow the presbytery as you would the Apostles; reverence the deacons as you would God's commandment. Let no one do anything touching the Church, apart from the bishop. Let that celebration of the Eucharist be considered valid which is held under the bishop or anyone to whom he has committed it. Where the bishop appears, there let the people be, just as where Jesus Christ is, there is the Catholic Church.[6]

Similarly, Ignatius wrote to the Trallians:

2. Surely, when you submit to the bishop as representing Jesus Christ, it is clear to me that you are not living the life of men, but that of Jesus Christ, who died for us, that through faith in His death you might escape dying. It is needful, then—and such is your practice—that you do nothing without your bishop; but be subject also to the presbytery as representing the Apostles of Jesus Christ, *our hope*, in whom we are expected to live forever. It is further necessary that the deacons, the dispensers of the mysteries of Jesus Christ, should win the approval of all in every way; for they are not dispensers of food and drink, but ministers of a church of God.[7]

It is also telling that Ignatius writes from the understanding of the fundamental unity of bishop, presbyters and deacons; he is constantly referring his readers to submit to them; as he wrote to the Ephesians, "so that you, fully trained in unanimous submission, may be submissive to the bishop and the presbytery, and thus be sanctified in every respect."[8]

---

5   (Peabody, MA: Hendrickson Publishers, 1997) p. 97.
6   *The Epistles of St. Clement of Rome and St. Ignatius of Antioch*, trans. by James A. Kleist, (Westminster, MD: The Newman Press, 1961) p. 93.
7   ibid., p. 75–6.
8   ibid., p. 61.

It is perhaps difficult to directly relate the threefold office set forth in Ignatius' epistles to our present circumstances; Ignatius' clearly found the unity in the office of bishop expressed primarily in his teaching, and in the celebration of the Lord's Supper, not in later notions regarding the apostolic succession. Even deacons were declared to be "dispensers of the mysteries of Jesus Christ". The 'monarchial episcopate' of Ignatius thus resists rash questions, such as, "Which grade is most like our pastors?" One might well say: "All of them." Speaking of the office of the holy ministry as *episcopos*, one thing which is deserving of attention throughout Ignatius' epistles is the emphasis on "submission" to bishop, presbyter *and* deacon—rightly submitting to one office, is to be in submission to all. Hierarchical submission is set forth as intrinsic to the unity of the Church: "Hence it is proper for you to act in agreement with the mind of the bishop; and this you do. Certain it is that your presbytery, which is a credit to its name, is a credit to God; for it harmonizes with the bishop as completely as the strings with a harp. This is why in the symphony of your concord and love the praises of Jesus Christ are sung." (Ephesians.4)[9] Again, as Ignatius wrote to Polycarp: "My life is a ransom for those who are obedient to the bishop, presbyters, and deacons; and in their company may I obtain my portion! Toil together, wrestle together, run together, suffer together, rest together, rise together, since you are stewards in God's house, members of His household, and His servants." (6.1)[10]

Reading Ignatius, it is hard not to think of the words of of Hebrews 13: "Remember those who rule over you, who have spoken the word of God to you, whose faith follow, considering the outcome of their conduct." (v. 7) Again, "Obey those who rule over you, and be submissive, for they watch

---

9   ibid.
10   ibid., p. 98.

out for your souls, as those who must give account. Let them do so with joy and not with grief, for that would be unprofitable for you." (v. 17) The submission which Ignatius upholds for the church toward bishops, presbyters, and deacons is that which is proclaimed in Hebrews 13 concerning the office of the holy ministry. If modern ears are made uncomfortable by the words of St. Ignatius—"submit to the bishop..."—perhaps the problem is the word "submit"; ours is not an age or culture which acknowledges willingly submitting to anything or anyone, and thus the order in all three God-given estates—Church, State and Home—is attacked. Ignatius' counsel to his fellow bishop, Polycarp— that is, "A Christian is not his own master; his time belongs to God" (7.3)—is something which neither the clergy nor laity want to hear in our generation. In a culture as devoted as our own to self-aggrandizement, any such a call for a godly submission or for self-sacrifice draw anger. Therefore, the call must be repeated more frequently, and more firmly.

I have singled out Ignatius because his threefold division of the one office of the ministry emphasizes a unity in doctrine which arises from unity in Word and Sacrament. For all of the differences between his time and our own, there is a common concern for a godly unity, and for Christ's ministers to be overseers of the flock, as the Lord of the Church has called them to be. I believe that the remnant which lives among the ruins of what was once Christendom has much to learn from the saints before Constantine.

The Episcopate and the Office of the Holy Ministry in the Book of Concord

At this point, we turn our eyes to the office of overseer as it is set forth in the Book of Concord. There was a conscious intention among the reformers to return *ad fontes* to the Holy Scriptures and church fathers (when their exposition of the

Scriptures was a correct one), and so perhaps we are justified in not devoting the attention to developments regarding the office of the holy ministry prior to that point as we might otherwise desire to do, if time permitted.

Returning to a point which was addressed above in our cursory examination the New Testament office of overseer, a consistent theme throughout the Book of Concord with regard to the office of the holy ministry is that there is one divinely established office; *iure humano* various grades have been introduced within the holy office, nevertheless it remains true that *iure divino* there remains one office. When the work of this holy ministry is described at any length (such as may be found in AC XXVIII, AP XXVIII and the Treatise) the reformers fairly pointedly unite the various 'grades' within a single description of the labors of the holy ministry which is inclusive of the work given to all ministers. Thus, for example, we read in Article XXVIII of the Augsburg Confession: "But this is their opinion, that the power of the Keys, or the power of the bishops, according to the Gospel, is a power or commandment of God, to preach the Gospel, to remit and retain sins, and to administer sacraments. For with that commandment, Christ sends forth his Apostles [John 20:21sqq.]: 'As my Father has sent me, even so send I you. Receive ye the Holy Ghost. Whosoever sins ye remit, they are remitted unto them; and whosoever sins ye retain, they are retained.'" (§5-6) The ministry is thus the apostolic ministry, and the power of the bishops is the power of the keys.

> Again, according to the Gospel, or as they say, according to Divine Law, to the bishop as bishops, that is, to those to whom has been committed the ministry of the Word and the sacraments, no jurisdiction belongs except to forgive sins, to discern doctrine, to reject doctrines contrary to the Gospel, and to exclude from the communion of the Church wicked men, whose wickedness is known, and this without human force, simply by the Word. Herein the congregations

are bound by Divine Law to obey them, according to Luke 10:16: "He that heareth you, heareth me." (§21–22)

Although the office of bishop is emphasized, the unity *iure divino* of the one office of the holy ministry is emphasized in the manner in which the episcopal office is defined; that is, in terms primarily of Word and Sacrament and jurisdiction, which are common to all those whom Christ has called to the holy office. Thus, as was observed in the author's January 2005 essay, "Pastoral Responsibility and the Office of the Keys in the Book of Concord": "Throughout the Lutheran Confessions, the link between the office of the keys and pastoral responsibility is expressed primarily on the parish level. The episcopate may be established as a visible (even preferable) representation of the unity of those united in doctrine and practice. But the Lutheran Confessions clearly teach that the bishop *does not* possess any higher authority with regard to pastoral jurisdiction."[11] Again, it is as we read in the Treatise:

> The Gospel has assigned to those who preside over churches the command to teach the Gospel, to remit sins, to administer the sacraments, and besides jurisdiction, viz. the command to excommunicate those whose crimes are known, and again of absolving the repenting.
>
> And by the confession of all, even of the adversaries, it is clear that this power by divine right is common to all who preside over churches, whether they be called pastors, or presbyters, or bishops. (§60-61)

By this definition, the Lutheran Confessions also clearly uphold that bishops are within the only holy office: the work which Christ Jesus has given to them to do is that which is common to all those in the ministry. The Lutheran Confessions clearly uphold that it is the calling of bishops to preach the Word and administer the Sacraments—just like all other called and ordained servants of the Word. This unity

---

11   See p. 140 of this volume.

of office can be seen in the labor which the Treatise identifies as one which is particularly associated with the episcopate: ordination. Melanchthon asks,

> For with the exception of ordination, what does the bishop that the presbyter does not? Jerome therefore teaches that it is by human authority that the grades of bishop and presbyter or pastor are distinct. And the subject itself declares this, because the power is the same, as he has said above. But one matter afterwards made a distinction between bishops and pastors, viz. ordination, because it was so arranged that one bishop might ordain ministers in a number of churches. But since by divine authority the grades of bishop and pastor are not diverse, it is manifest that ordination by a pastor in his own church has been appointed by divine law.
>
> Therefore, when the regular bishops become enemies of the Church, or are unwilling to administer ordination, the churches retain their own right. (§62–65)

There is an important tension contained within this passage, in particular, in the treatment of the episcopal grade throughout the Book of Concord. On the one hand, the Confessions clearly uphold that by divine institution, the authority given to the holy ministry is common to all who are called to that office, regardless of human distinction of grade; even the particular work of ordination may be carried out by a pastor within his own church, "by divine law." However, the Lutherans sought to avoid schismatic practices with regard to ordination: "*when* the regular bishops become enemies of the Church, or are *unwilling* to administer ordination, the churches retain their own right."

The authors of the Lutheran Confessions unfeignedly sought to avoid schism, and to render due obedience, to those who, *iure humano*, had authority over them. Thus, for example, the express concern at the conclusion of AC XXVIII: "But the bishops might easily retain the lawful obedience of the people, if they would not insist upon the the observance

of such traditions as cannot be kept with a good conscience."
(§69) The Treatise rightly protests,

> Since, therefore, bishops have tyrannically transferred this
> jurisdiction [excommunication] to themselves alone, and
> have basely abused it, there is no need, because of this
> jurisdiction, to obey bishops. But since the reasons why we do
> not obey are just, it is right also to restore this jurisdiction to
> godly pastors, and to see to it that it be legitimately exercised
> for the reformation of life and the glory of God. (§76)

Also the words of Apology XIV ought to be taken at face value,
and not treated as some sort of deception, when Melanchthon
wrote: "we have frequently testified in this assembly that it is
our greatest wish to maintain Church polity and the grades
in the Church, even through they have been made by human
authority. For we know that Church discipline was instituted
by the Fathers, in the manner laid down in the ancient canons,
with a good and useful intention." (§24) Again,

> Furthermore, we wish here again to testify that we will glad-
> ly maintain ecclesiastical and canonical order, provided the
> bishops only cease to rage against our Churches. This our
> desire will clear us both before God and among all nations
> to all posterity from the imputation against us, that the au-
> thority of the bishops is being undermined, when men read
> and hear, that, although protesting against the unrighteous
> cruelty of the bishops, we could not obtain justice. (§28)

All this being said, if we are to consider the "future
of ecclesiastical oversight" in the Lutheran Church, then we
ought first to consider it where it is primarily to be found: in
the Church gathered around Word and Sacrament, in which
the Lord of the Church has called a man to be an overseer of
the flock, to bind and loose sins, and to be the steward of the
mysteries of God. In the proper sense, this is *episcopé*, which
the Lutheran Confessions call "jurisdiction," or the "power of
the keys."

The keys have been obscured by bylaws, convention resolutions, CTCR documents, congregational constitutions, etc. But the responsibility remains, because the institution of the holy office remains.

The Gospel has assigned to those who preside over churches the command to teach the Gospel, to remit sins, to administer the sacraments, and besides jurisdiction, viz. the command to excommunicate those whose crimes are known, and again of absolving the repenting.

> And by the confession of all, even of the adversaries, it is clear that this power by divine right is common to all who preside over churches, whether they be called pastors, or presbyters, or bishops. (§60-61)

The author has, on occasion, heard from those who believe that the solution to the Church's troubles is the need for a "synodical official" who can step into the congregation and "deal" with problems that arise therein, and deliver the pastor from his troubles. I say, what is needed is for pastors to once again take up the responsibility of being overseers of the flock. As the office of the holy ministry is, *iure divino*, one office, "ecclesiastical oversight" within the congregation is the calling of the pastor, to oversee the Church within the place to which the Lord of the Church has called him. This responsibility from God does not mitigate against willing submission, one unto another, among ministers of Christ's Church for the sake of good order. Thus there is a manifest desire to testify before God and man that the Lutheran confessors did not seek to seize anything which belonged to the grade of bishop. Their actions against the episcopal grade were only defensible in light of the necessities implicit in the Lord's institution of the one office of the holy ministry.

Ecclesiastical Oversight in the Early Reformation

The 1528 Saxon Visitation

The actions of the Lutheran fathers regarding the canonical bishops of the Roman Church were necessary for the sake of the Gospel. But the "greatest wish" to maintain the polity of the Church was not an empty claim among the Lutherans; it found expression even before Augsburg in the establishment of the office of Superintendent. Although the word "Superintendent" has gained its own peculiar usage in modern English, it is, nonetheless, simply the Latin term equivalent to *episcopos*, meaning "overseer." Thus when Luther and Melanchthon wrote the "Instructions for the Visitors of Parish Pastors in Electoral Saxony" in 1527/1528, the office of Superintendent was described in terms of episcopal ecclesiastical oversight. Thus Luther began the Preface to the "Instructions":

> Both the Old and the New Testaments give sufficient evidence of what a divinely wholesome thing it would be if pastors and Christian congregations might be visited by understanding and competent persons. For we read in Acts 9 [:32] that St. Peter traveled about in the land of the Jews. And in Acts 15 [:2] we are told that St. Paul together with Barnabas revisited all those places where they had preached. All his epistles reveal his concern for all the congregations and pastors. He writes letters, he sends his disciples, he goes himself.[12]

In fact, Luther declared that Christ Jesus was the model above any other of the role of Superintendent within the Church: "More than any, Christ has done this kind of work on behalf of all, and on this account possessed no place on earth where he could lay his head or which he could call his own. This began even while he was in the womb, for he went with his mother over the hills to visit St. John [Luke 1:39]."[13] This is an

---

12   in *Luther's Works*, 55 vols., vol. 40 (Fortress Press, 1958) p. 269.
13   ibid.

amazing claim, to be sure, but we would do well to consider the reaction of St. John to this visit by his *Episcopos*:

> And it happened, when Elizabeth heard the greeting of Mary, that the babe leaped in her womb; and Elizabeth was filled with the Holy Spirit. Then she spoke out with a loud voice and said, "Blessed are you among women, and blessed is the fruit of your womb! But why is this granted to me, that the mother of my Lord should come to me? For indeed, as soon as the voice of your greeting sounded in my ears, the babe leaped in my womb for joy. Blessed is she who believed, for there will be a fulfillment of those things which were told her from the Lord." (Luke 1:41:45)

Luther set forth the visitation as the most important ongoing aspect of the work of bishops, declaring that

> Formerly, in the days of the ancient Fathers, the holy bishops diligently followed these examples and even yet much of this is found in the papal laws. For it was in this kind of activity that the bishops and archbishops had their origin—each one was obligated to a greater or lesser extent to visit and examine. For, actually, bishop means supervisor or visitor, and archbishop a supervisor or visitor of bishops, to see to it that each parish pastor visits and watches over and supervises his people in regard to teaching and life. And the archbishop was to visit, watch over, and supervise the bishops as to their teaching.[14]

In other words, in Luther's estimation, as the pastor is *episcopos* to his congregation, so the bishop is *episcopos* to the pastors of his diocese, and the archbishop is *episcopos* to the bishops of his archdiocese. Luther bemoaned the fact that "so worthy an office"[15] had deteriorated until "nothing remained of it except the burdening and banning of people because of money, debts, and temporal goods and the making of a divine order out of the bellowing of antiphons and versicles in churches. No attention is paid to how one teaches, believes, loves, how one lives a Christian life, how to care for the poor, how one

14   ibid., p. 269–270.
15   ibid., p. 270.

comforts the weak, or punishes the unruly, and whatever else belongs to such an office."[16] The manifest intention of the Saxon Visitation was to address such a need for ecclesiastical oversight, and the "Instructions" addressed the appointment of Superintendents so that such a need would be met on an ongoing basis in the future.

The work of the visitors to bring unity was not to be despised by the pastors: "We hope they will not ungratefully and proudly despise our love and good intention, but will willingly, without any compulsion, subject themselves in a spirit of love to such visitations and with us peacefully accept these visitors until God the Holy Spirit brings to pass something that is better, through them or through us."[17] However, "If some obstinately want to set themselves against us and without good reason demand something else, as there always are undisciplined heads who out of utter perversity are able to do nothing in common or in agreement, but are different and self-centered in heart and life, we must separate these from ourselves as chaff on the threshing floor and refuse to accommodate ourselves to them."[18] Truly, an astounding demand of submission to such visitors. The authority of the Visitors—and, later, the Superintendents—was not to be despised; those who insisted on rebellion "out of their perversity" were to be marked and avoided.

It was to be the role of the Superintendents to fulfill the responsibility of visitation in the future. As the "Instructions" declare concerning "The Office of Superintendent":

> This pastor (*Pfarrherr*) shall be superintendent of all the other priests who have their parish or benefice in the region, whether they live in monasteries or foundations of nobles or of others. He shall make sure that in these parishes there is correct Christian teaching, that the Word of God and the holy gospel are truly and purely proclaimed,

16   ibid.
17   ibid., p. 272–273.
18   ibid., p. 273.

184

and that the holy sacraments according to the institution of Christ are provided to the blessing of the people.[19]

Thus it is observed that the Superintendent is a pastor—he holds the same divine office as those whom he supervises, though of a different grade of ministry, by human rite. The responsibility of the Superintendent was to assure that the *nota ecclesiae* were upheld among all ministers "in the region"—consistently a diocesan understanding of the Church. Future candidates for ministry were to be directed to the Superintendent;

> We have also considered it wise to ordain that in the future when a pastor or preacher either by death or otherwise leaves his benefice and some one is accepted in his place by the patron, such a one shall be presented to the superintendent before he is given the benefice or received as a preacher. The superintendent shall question and examine him as to his life and teaching and whether he will satisfactorily serve the people, so that by God's help we may carefully prevent any ignorant or incompetent person from being accepted and unlearned folk being misled. (313–4)

Clearly, the Superintendents were the 'gatekeepers'—stopping unfit men from being installed as pastors, and removing those who were unworthy of their office.

The model of Visitation and work of the Superintendent set forth in the "Instructions" was consistently upheld by Luther as the Reformation progressed; a second edition of the "Instructions" was printed in 1538, and Bugenhagen published a Latin edition of the "Instructions" as part of his reorganization of the Danish Church in 1538. Luther also wrote a preface in 1545 for an edition used by the diocese of Naumberg.[20] This model of the office of superintendent was also adopted elsewhere, e.g. in Hesse.

In Hesse the office of superintendent was established in 1531. The territory was divided into six districts,

---

19   ibid., p. 313.
20   ibid., p. 267.

each with a Superintendent who exercised ecclesiastical jurisdiction over all within his area. Together with the "most learned and fit pastors" their gathering in a synod represented the highest ecclesiastical authority in the territory. The *Kirchendienerordnung* of 1531 and that of 1537 described the specific responsibilities of the Superintendent, such as visiting all the pastors in the district once a year.[21]

The Superintendency of Martin Chemnitz

The "Second Martin"—Martin Chemnitz (1522–1586)—upheld the same teaching regarding ecclesiastical oversight as that which was expounded by Martin Luther. Chemnitz was actually called to serve in the office of Superintendent, being the fourth to hold that office in Braunschweig since the beginning of the Reformation.[22] Preus observes that the use of the keys—church discipline—was of particular importance to Chemnitz as it pertained to ecclesiastical oversight within the parishes of Braunschweig; "he wanted a clear area for the church to determine its teaching and carry out its discipline, unmolested by the state, yet supported by it. He does not call upon the state to punish the sins of Christian church members but rather to let the church set its own ecclesiastical penalties."

Chemnitz was "unanimously called" to the office of Superintendent on September 20, 1567. Within four days, Chemnitz submitted specific proposals for the fulfillment of his office, and these proposals were also unanimously approved. Chemnitz specifically required of the clergy of his superintendency: "And just as we preach and teach the positive points in the one Spirit, so we will all fight on the same side in necessary controversies and stand together against errors, and when new conflicts arise, we will not each follow his own judgment and personal opinion but rather will deliberate to-

---

21   Ralph F. Smith, *Luther, Ministry, and Ordination Rites in the Early Reformation Church*, (New York: Peter Lang, 1996) p. 147

22   J.A.O. Preus, *The Second Martin*, (St. Louis: Concordia Publishing House, 1994) p. 131.

gether in conference over the points under controversy."[23] Not only uniformity in doctrine, but in church practices would be expected:

> Likewise, we must all stick together, as we have in the past, and retain the practice that each does not build up himself or act as lord in his congregation and do what he pleases in preaching, administration of the sacraments, liturgical practices, discipline and the other aspects of his office, acting only according to his own ideas, but rather all these things shall be and remain the business of the entire ministerium."[24]

The city council would not interfere regarding the *corpus doctrinae*, nor church discipline.[25] No interference in church discipline would be tolerated: "The honorable council will not hinder church discipline but rather help support it, since the binding key is a necessary part of the ministry."[26] No call into the holy ministry would be extended "without the consent of the superintendent and the ministerium."[27]

Conclusion

This brief survey has allowed an opportunity to consider the understanding of ecclesiastical oversight set forth in Holy Scripture and the Book of Concord (1580), and the application of that responsibility within several of the early Lutheran superintendencies of Germany. More could be said regarding such oversight, particularly in those areas where the episcopate was more directly preserved, particularly among the archbishops and bishops of Scandinavia.

"Ecclesiastical oversight" is, in its most primary sense,

---

23   ibid., p. 133.
24   ibid.
25   ibid., p. 134–135.
26   ibid., p. 136.
27   ibid.

the God-given responsibility of the pastor to be the steward of the mysteries of God in the congregation to which the Lord of the Church has called him to serve. This ministry necessarily includes jurisdiction—that is, binding and loosing sins—in the stead and by the command of Christ. But ecclesiastical oversight has also included an episcopal office of Bishop or Superintendent from the earliest days of Christendom, through the period of Reformation Orthodoxy. Luther clearly maintained that such oversight was part of the regular life of the Church, and the Lutheran Confessions upheld even the retaining of canonical polity as of great importance to the Lutheran Church. These facts are of critical importance to confessional Lutherans in our own age. Christians of our confession understand themselves to be in a diaspora in this age, and the exercise of oversight is not easily accomplished. Certainly there is a great willingness—both within the synods and without—to "go one's own way." We would do well to heed the voices of our fathers in the faith, and seek a godly oversight, free from the tyranny of our modern successors to the Roman bishops—whose conduct proved that they were not, in fact, bishops at all. What is needed today is the visible unity of ecclesiastical oversight within and among confessional Lutheran parishes and their pastors.

Soli Deo Gloria